AF599244

DARE TO OWN You

Dare to Own You

"*Dare to Own You* is a wonderful book that opens your mind and your heart. Liz offers you tools to learn how to determine what you really want in life, and how to then achieve more, and faster, than you ever thought possible. This book can change your life."

~ **Brian Tracy**, International Speaker, bestselling Author, Consultant

"In *Dare to Own You*, Liz Brunner shares powerful insights about how to look for the lessons and gifts in every life situation. This book offers powerful wisdom and thoughtful questions that invite you to look at your life from a new perspective, go after your dreams, and celebrate everything you have to give to this world."

~ **Marci Shimoff**, #1 *New York Times* bestselling author, *Happy for No Reason* and *Chicken Soup for the Woman's Soul*

"Sitting next to Liz at the anchor desk in Boston, her curiosity, her kindness, her care for others was always on full display, but I'm convinced what fueled it all was something inside her. Liz has long carried a quiet strength, a sense of self, and an undying spirit. Anyone embarking on their next chapter will benefit from Liz's honesty, determination, and her willingness to bring others with her. Liz is proof the keys to true personal growth and brilliant next chapters come from untapped power within."

~ **David Muir**, Anchor, *ABC World News Tonight with David Muir*

"I've had the opportunity to get to know Liz Brunner over the past few years and have witnessed her transformation from award-winning news anchor, to a highly successful communications coach and expert in her field. In her book, *Dare to Own You*, Liz does a masterful job of sharing her own personal journey, while offering practical tools to help people overcome limiting beliefs and sustain positive behavioral changes to achieve more success.

~ **Dr. Marshall Goldsmith**, two-time Thinkers 50 #1 Leadership Thinker in the World, #1 *New York Times* bestselling author of *Triggers*, *MOJO* and *What Got You Here Won't Get You There*

"At some point, it's almost certain that everyone will need to reinvent themselves. In *Dare to Own You*, Liz Brunner shares her own impressive career journey and provides a tangible framework to help you discover your next chapter. Learn to tap into your own unique strengths, make a powerful contribution, and to transform your life and career!"

~ **Dorie Clark**, author of *Reinventing You* and executive education faculty, Duke University Fuqua School of Business

"You never have to question something that is real, and Liz Brunner is the real deal! Her compelling story in *Dare to Own You* will guide you on how to endure the storms of life, find your authentic voice, believe in your dreams and claim your power and purpose. *Dare to Own You* will take you on a powerful journey of self-discovery to become more of who you are meant to be."

~ **Trent Shelton**, Motivational Speaker, Author, Founder and President of RehabTime and former NFL Wide Receiver

"Compelling. Insightful. Inspiring. In *Dare to Own You*, Liz Brunner's powerful storytelling offers you an invitation to give yourself permission to be your authentic self, live your passion and purpose, and when you do, you have the opportunity to make your dreams come true."

~**Patty Aubery**, #1 *New York Times* bestselling Author, Co-Founder & President of The Canfield Training Group, and CVO GOALFriends Global

"There's an important message for everyone in *"Dare to Own You."* Liz Brunner's journey weaves together subtle lessons about courage, leadership, determination, resilience and perseverance. What emerges is an approach to life that will empower the reader to reach their fullest potential and tap into their authentic spirit. Hooyah!"

~ **Commander Mark Divine**, retired Navy SEAL, founder of SEALFIT and Unbeatable Mind, and New York Times bestselling author, *The Way of The SEAL*

"Dare to Own You will inspire and encourage you to fully embrace your light and claim your highest path. Filled with wisdom and guidance, Liz Brunner will help you discern the distinction between a wish and a dream, honor your power of being vulnerable, and show you how to put your own energy into action to create positive change in your life! Liz's years of experience and insight shine throughout!"

~ **Laura Lynne Jackson**, *New York Times* bestselling Author, *Signs* and *The Light Between Us*

"Liz takes the reader on an intimate thought-provoking journey of what is possible if you dare to own YOU. A fabulous read!"

~ **Annette Comer**, bestselling author *Rescue Me*, Founder World's Greatest Women Leadership Platform

"With warmth, encouragement, and thought-provoking prompts, Liz Brunner's beautiful book will help you build confidence, connect with your unique voice, and share your best gifts with the world."

~ **Jenny Blake**, Author and Podcast Host of *Free Time* and *Pivot*

"The difference between those that do, and those that do not, has very little to do with talent and everything to do with belief. In *Dare to Own You,* Liz Brunner helps you to remember all of who you are, and gives you reflection exercises to guide you to discover all of who you have yet to be. This book will be your 'go to!'"

~**Petra Kolber**, Speaker, Podcast Host and Author, *The Perfection Detox: Tame Your Inner Critic, Live Bravely, and Unleash Your Joy*

DARE TO OWN

Taking Your Authenticity and Dreams into Your Next Chapter

Liz Brunner

Dare to Own You
Taking Your Authenticity and Dreams into Your Next Chapter

First edition published 2021
Second edition published 2025

The information in this book is a truthful recollection of actual events in the author's life. The names and identifying characteristics of individuals and places may have been changed to maintain anonymity.

GracePoint Matrix, LLC
624 S. Cascade Ave Suite 201, Colorado Springs, CO 80903
www.GracePointMatrix.com
Admin@GracePointMatrix.com

SAN # 991-6032
Library of Congress Control Number: 2021918170

ISBN: (Hardback) 978-1-961347-84-7
eISBN: (eBook) 978-1-951694-79-1

Books may be purchased for educational, business, or sales promotional use.
For distribution queries contact Sales@IPGbook.com
For non-retail bulk order requests contact Orders@GracePointPublishing.com

This book is dedicated to my mom,
Mary Chacko Russell.
Your generous spirit, unconditional love and support,
and wisdom have guided me
from chapter to chapter of my life.
Thank you!
I love you and am blessed to be your daughter.

ACKNOWLEDGMENTS

Writing this book has been truly a labor of love and I feel so grateful to many who encouraged me along the way.

Thank you to my family, friends and yes, even my "foes," for you all taught me lessons along the way. No knowledge—or experience—is ever wasted and I wouldn't be where I am today without your love, support and acceptance, and for challenging me to learn and grow.

Thank you to my team at Brunner Communications. When you surround yourself with good people, it makes everyone better, and all of you have done that with me and for me.

To my clients. Working with all of you has brought me enormous joy and given me confidence in my goal to truly help people find their voice and be their best self no matter what industry you are in.

To my business coach, Michelle Vandepas, thank you for guiding me to focus my energy professionally and personally, to realize what my vision for my life is: to teach, motivate and inspire people to live their best life. You came into my life at the perfect time and I truly believe we were meant to work together. I am blessed to know you and have worked with you.

Shauna Hardy, my writing coach, you believed in me from the get-go and encouraged me to own more of who I am in my writing. The more I wrote, the more I had to say, and it was because of you. To Laurie Miller Knight, whose editing expertise was invaluable!

To everyone at GracePoint Publishing. I couldn't have written my first book without your encouragement and support every step of the way. You made what felt like a daunting process (and it is!) into one that was manageable and made me feel like "yes, I can do this."

A huge thank you to my podcast guests: I am grateful for your authenticity in bearing your souls to me and our listeners all around the world. Your stories have allowed people to realize that they too can grow. They can create a next chapter and live their best life. It has been an honor to connect with you.

Without all of you in my life, there would be no book.

And last but not least, I give thanks to God, the universe, source, whatever you call your higher power. My faith has guided me throughout my life, and I truly believe with every fiber of my being that you helped me write this book. Sharing some of my most vulnerable experiences was scary, surreal and liberating at the same time. I pray with all my heart that it will guide others to own who they are.

FOREWORD

Before you dive into the pages of this book, I want to encourage you to think about the goals that you are dreaming of achieving in your life. Perhaps you are thinking about switching careers, starting a new business, building a dream home, or connecting with the love of your life. Perhaps you wish to create more time in your schedule so that you have the freedom to truly enjoy your days in the manner of your choosing.

All of the dreams that I mentioned have one common ingredient. In order for them to become a reality, they all require your total commitment. Commitment is the enduring quality that steadily moves the needle toward achieving what we want in our lives. When obstacles occur, when faith wavers, when fatigue kicks in, it is our unwavering commitment to ourselves and to our dreams that keeps us marching forward on the path toward success.

So, how committed are you?

When I first connected with Liz as a guest on her podcast, I was impressed by her commitment to her craft and her commitment to helping others become their most authentic selves. Throughout all the stories that she shares in *Dare to Own You*, it is clear that Liz is fully committed to living life to its biggest, brightest, and fullest potential. With each "next chapter" she builds upon her knowledge and her experience, continually moving herself forward and expanding her world as she creates the life of her dreams. From music teacher to award-winning broadcast journalist to the CEO of Brunner Communications, Liz has learned the power of connecting fully to her authentic self and expressing it to the world.

My hope is that in reading this book you too will be inspired by her story to take the actions that will make *your* dreams come true.

And here is the most important point… *Dare to Own You* is not a book to be read and put back on a shelf. This book is offering you the possibility of a powerful transformation in your life. As you read, I am asking you to make the commitment to fully engage and complete the reflective exercises that are featured at the end of each chapter. The answers to these questions hold the keys to creating a deeply enriching life for yourself. I truly hope you will do yourself the favor of investing that time and making that commitment. I promise you the extra effort will be well worth it.

Here's to your success and to creating your next amazing chapter!

—Jack Canfield

Co-creator of the *Chicken Soup for the Soul®* series and *The Success Principles™: How to Get from Where You Are to Where You Want to Be*

CONTENTS

INTRODUCTION (SECOND EDITION)

I want to take a moment to thank you for choosing to read my book, but not for the reason you may think. While I am honored to share my story with you, I want to thank you for giving yourself permission and for making time to take yourself on an authentic journey, to get out of your comfort zone, to overcome some of your limiting beliefs, and to transform your life. If I can find the courage to do it—and to keep doing it—I believe you can too.

My grandmother, Dr. Dorothy Chacko, whom you will meet in these pages, was fond of saying, "No knowledge is ever wasted." There is such truth in that quote. You know more than you think you know, learn to trust that.

With each chapter, I share a part of my journey and the insights I gained along the way, and I invite you to reflect on your own life—on all your experiences, both the highs and the lows—to connect the dots and discover what themes and patterns emerge.

Remember: All of your experiences and the knowledge you gained have shaped and molded you, and those are your stories. Take the time to reflect on them and within that reflection, you will find your purpose and your truth.

May the stories of my journey inspire you to dig deeply, to discover your dreams, to dare to own who you are, and live your best life, whatever that means for you.

With love and appreciation,

Liz

Own Your Authenticity

SECTION ONE

1

No Knowledge is Ever Wasted

What would you attempt to do if you knew you could not fail?

~ Robert Schuller

Jumping Off a Cliff

It's the day after Christmas, 2015. It's a cool but sunny morning in Southern California. I did something I had always wanted to do but took it off my bucket list, thinking it was a foolish idea. I was too old for such nonsense. What did I do? I jumped out of an airplane and went skydiving for the first time in my life. Free falling from 13,000 feet at 120 mph for the first sixty seconds was both exhilarating and terrifying, all at the same time! Because I didn't bend my legs at the knees as my stepson had told me to do, I did a complete "180," which is not what you are supposed to do.

"Don't forget to breathe." That advice was given to me by a solo jumper just prior to my crawling onto the floor of our open-door airplane. Her words echoed in my head as I did my somersault in the air. *Just breathe,*

Liz, just breathe. I began laughing to myself because ironically that is what I am always telling my clients to do. Just breathe!

Thanks to my tandem jumper—to whom I was securely attached—once he had me pull my parachute, the remaining minutes of our descent to *terra firma* were peaceful and beautiful. I could see up and down the entire west coast.

I didn't know I was an entrepreneur until I became one.

As scary as jumping out of an airplane was, even scarier was starting my own business. That truly felt like jumping off a cliff and hoping I had a parachute. At least when I went skydiving, I did have a parachute. You see, I never, ever had an interest in starting a business.

Yet, in some ways, I feel I've come full circle. As an adolescent, I lovingly coerced Grammie into giving me her blank watermarked stationery, and using my colored pencils and markers, I drew pretty flowers on them. Once my artistry was complete, I went around selling them for five cents a page to our neighbors at our rented summer cottage at Lake Howe, Indiana. My other business endeavors were a few lemonade stands, a newspaper route, my babysitting gigs, and what young Brownie or Girl Scout didn't sell cookies for her troop?

Take the Risk

I guess I am an entrepreneur at heart. I just didn't know it, that is, until I became one. Being an entrepreneur is not for the faint of heart. It involves taking a risk, a big risk! I never really thought of myself as a risk-taker until I jumped out of that airplane, but in hindsight, I've also come to realize that I am more of a risk-taker than I ever thought.

Music was a big part of my life growing up, whether singing in the church choir, my Pekin High School show choir, The Noteables, or in the Peoria Civic Opera Company. Our family was like the Von Trapps of our community, singing in nursing homes and, of course, in church. It never occurred to me that I should study anything other than music.

During my senior year in high school, our concert choir participated in the Midstate 9 Choir Festival. Choirs from our entire district were brought together as one group. Our conductor was Dr. Karle Erikson from Lawrence University. From the moment he entered the auditorium and jumped up on stage for our first rehearsal with this massive ensemble, his energy and aura were infectious! *OMG! I want to sing for him every day.* THIS is where I would go to school! It was the only school I applied to. Talk about taking a risk!

Lawrence was a private university in Appleton, Wisconsin. It was also very expensive. So expensive that my father thought I should live at home and go to a junior college nearby. No way was I going to do that! I was not going to the local college, and I was not going to live at home! (Appleton was about an eight-hour drive from my home in Pekin, Illinois.) I was determined to find a way to get all the money I would need.

I have always been very proud of the fact that I paid for all my college education. Between my summer jobs, babysitting money, the pageant scholarship money, government student loans (which took years to pay off), and working in the dish room of our on-campus cafeteria, I did it.

Upon graduating from Lawrence University Conservatory of Music, I got a job teaching high school choral music at Rich South High School in Richton Park, Illinois. In my first year, I was honored to lead four choirs, including one swing-show choir. I was also responsible for monitoring a dreaded study hall.

Away from the classroom, I found much joy singing with a semi-professional chorale, the Park Forest Singers, based outside of Chicago. We performed several concerts every year, and even toured Europe, singing in Italy in the great cathedrals in Venice, Rome, at the Vatican, and all over Greece, Germany, and Switzerland. For a couple of years, that was my life, teaching and singing in the chorale, but deep down, as much as I loved teaching music, I knew two years in—organically, deep within my soul—that there was something "more" I was supposed to do. I felt like there was a "next chapter." I couldn't explain it, nor did I have a clue as to what I wanted it to be. When my contract ended, I left.

Little did I know that all that musical and vocal training would play such a big role in my future. Certainly not in the way one might expect.

Next Stop: TV!

"No knowledge is ever wasted." The number of times those words were spoken at home! They penetrated my ears growing up. They came from my mother and her mother, Grandmother Chacko.

Although, truth be told, Grandmother would say, "No knowledge is ever wasted in the good Lord's sight." (That's the complete quote.) Those words still echo in my head today. They are what got me to where I am right now. They were also the impetus for writing this book.

When I left teaching, I had no real clear path in sight. So, I returned to a high school passion of fashion. I worked in retail, selling clothes at Caren Charles to help pay the bills. I was good at it too. I became one of their top salespeople, making my way into their $100,000 Club my first year. But I still hadn't found my passion, nor what I thought was my purpose.

No knowledge is ever wasted.

I was reading all kinds of books on subjects in which I was interested. *Construction, yes, construction! Maybe I could be an architect?* I loved drawing floor plans. Or maybe I could become a psychologist. I was taking all kinds of assessment tests, trying to determine what my next chapter should be, what I might be good at. This was before the days of easy access to the internet. Nothing was resonating just yet.

I began reading the book *Who's Hiring Who* by Richard Lathrop. In it, he espouses the numerous advantages and opportunities that come from *informational interviews*. I'd never heard of such a thing, but it gave me an idea.

What about television? Where did THAT idea come from?

Television always fascinated me from the time we got our first black and white set, to watching the landing on the moon, to so many remarkable, historical events, all coming right into our living room.

During my reign as Miss Illinois 1979, I had done one TV commercial for the Pontiac Grand Prix, my favorite car at the time. The fact that I got to drive four different Grand Prix during my one-year reign was a fabulous perk, though I don't think I ever saw the commercial—if it even made it to the airwaves. That was the extent of my television experience, unless, of course, you count the live broadcast of the Miss America Pageant itself.

It was Lathrop's book that gave me the courage to consider television. I bravely and blindly called up the NBC and CBS affiliates in Champaign-Urbana, Illinois, and asked for an informational interview. *Did I have to go back to school? Did I have to have a degree in communications or journalism? Could I even get a job in television? Did the kind of job I thought I was interested in—public relations—even exist in television?* I had no idea what that meant! I didn't know who the right person was at either station to even ask any of those questions.

Thankfully, I was eventually connected with people who could answer them. Somehow, they agreed to meet me. I managed to get informational interviews at both TV stations. I seriously doubt that would happen today; the industry is far too competitive now.

After about six months of conversation back and forth with the CBS station, WCIA-TV, a position was created for me with the title of community relations liaison. (In case you're wondering, CIA does not stand for Central Intelligence Agency but rather Central

Illinois Area.) My job was to help coordinate all the public service announcements that went on the air, write and produce some of those spots, and coordinate our speakers' bureau.

I knew nothing! I had no clue how to do any of that. But I have always been a firm believer that just because I've never done something doesn't mean I can't. I just have to try.

I learned everything on the job. Whatever they asked me to do, I said yes! I said yes, no matter what, but then I'd go home and freak out in private. *Am I crazy for saying yes when I have no clue how to do anything they asked of me?* Probably, but again, I just had to try.

When we are all trying to do new things, no, we may not like some of the things we attempt to do, and no, we may not be good at them either. In fact, more than likely we won't be good at all of them, but we just learned what we don't like, which is almost as important as knowing what we *do* like.

With a lot of hard work and trepidation, I got better to the point where management made the decision to put my voice—just my voice and a few slides—on the air with the *Town Crier*, a 60-second spot highlighting events people might be interested in attending in the community. How I would fret every time I went into the sound booth; I was so nervous! Thankfully, more on-air, on-camera opportunities came from having my own little three-and-a-half-minute daily interview talk show, *Community Touch*, to being a weather person. Yes, I did the weather! We had a three-women weather team at that time, probably the only one in the country, I think.

To be certain I could, with confidence, talk about the weather—or at least **act** like I knew what I was talking about—I took a few meteorology courses at the University of Illinois and watched the weather channel before going into the studio. Once there, I studied every bit of AP (Associated Press) wire copy I could get my hands on to prepare my weather report. It was truly the best training one can have for live TV. There is no script.

I did learn to write scripts and edit them. Back then, we worked with three-quarter inch tape and created an "A-roll," the primary video, and a "B-roll," the supplemental video. I got real hands-on learning. That doesn't happen much these days in a "union" shop, where only the editors are allowed to touch the buttons. I am so grateful for all those opportunities to learn. It was my own graduate school.

What if they found out I was afraid?

Within a few years, I got a call from the owner of WTVT-13, the CBS affiliate in Tampa, Florida, looking for someone to fill a newly created position of community relations director. I got the job. I was the only female in upper management. Talk about taking a risk. *What if they found out I was scared? What if they found out I was afraid I couldn't do the job, didn't know how to do the job?* The "imposter syndrome" was in high gear! (I'll cover more of that in Chapter Two!) But I knew I had to somehow push past my fears to break through the glass ceiling that I felt existed, even if that meant faking it until I made it.

It wasn't long before they tapped me to be the morning news anchor, and oh yes, I was still expected to do my day job. I worked about eighty hours a week, getting up at 3:00 AM, going to work at 4:00 AM, on the air from 5:00 AM-7:00 AM, and working in the newsroom until 9:30 AM after the morning news meeting. I would then take my anchor hat off, put on my management hat, and head upstairs to my office for my other job. To say I was exhausted was an understatement, and yet, I pushed through.

It was not easy. I felt a bit ostracized by people in the newsroom who knew that because of my management role, I was privy to confidential information about the station, its direction, and yes, the people with whom I worked side by side in the newsroom. Can you blame them? Not at all!

With fatigue and exhaustion the main factors, after three years of that harrowing schedule, I *asked* to come off the air, off the anchor desk, and only do my community relations role. I told myself that if God wanted me back on the air, it would happen.

About a year later, out of the blue, it did. My agent called and said there was a highly successful news-magazine show called *Chronicle* at WCVB-TV, Channel 5, the ABC affiliate in Boston. They were interested in me being a correspondent and fill-in anchor.

I'd always felt Boston held some special place in my soul. *Was it because, as a child, one of our vacations was in Boston? Or perhaps because many of my ancestors landed on this east coast shore centuries ago, or was it because of this job?*

My interview went well, and I remember looking out the plane window on my flight back to Tampa knowing I would get offered the job and that my life was about to change, again. This was where

I was supposed to go. This was meant to be my next chapter. I took that leap of faith and moved, without knowing anyone in Boston.

I loved being on *Chronicle*! What a way to learn all about the rich history of New England and meet the people whose families, in some cases, had been there for generations.

This was big market TV. I was working alongside award-winning anchors, reporters, producers, videographers, and editors. The learning curve was steep and scary at times, but I loved it all.

Once again, I was asked to take on a second role, that of the morning *EyeOpener* news anchor… and yes, again, I would also continue working on *Chronicle*. I thought, *I've worn two hats at the same time before, I can do this*. (Did I have an invisible sign on my back that said, "Please give me two jobs to do at the same time"?)

What I didn't know until I was into both roles was that while *Chronicle* and the news department were a part of the same station, they had very different approaches to stories, and many in the highly competitive newsroom did not accept me at all. I didn't have the "Big J" (for journalist) on my chest. I was a nobody to them. In their minds, I didn't have the appropriate pedigree: no degree in journalism or communications. I was a music major.

There were days when I felt like I needed to wear a suit of armor to go into work because of the arrows I was sure were being thrown at my back. It was not easy. *They* didn't make it easy. But I loved the work; I loved telling stories. I pushed myself to learn and grow. Oh yeah, I fell flat on my face a few times—probably many times—

which certainly didn't help me in winning any of them over, nor did it help with my confidence. It was a struggle to maintain confidence, and sometimes I had a sense that "they" could almost smell it and took advantage of it. But I refused to give up. "They" (whoever all of the "they" were) were not going to get the best of me!

Those challenging experiences taught me some very important lessons about real confidence that I still use today and share with my clients. It takes courage to be confident. We must make the choice to be confident. And confidence is something we learn and continue to learn throughout our lifetime. (There's a lot more on this topic in Chapter Three.)

Through many different roles, and a tremendous amount of hard work, I did get better. Enough to be promoted to co-anchoring both the 5:30 PM and 11:00 PM newscast, and then I was moved to the #1 rated newscast in the market, the 6:00 PM show, replacing an icon. We sat at #1 in the Nielsen ratings for 135 consecutive months! By this time, though, the industry was changing dramatically. Stories were getting shorter in length and content, meaning they were not as in-depth as I liked them to be. The dynamics at the station were also evolving. More and more was being expected of each of us as anchors and reporters.

No longer was my schedule a given. I was being moved around to so many different shifts from week to week. My tenure didn't seem to matter either. The women anchoring the news were also getting younger and younger, and not only on my station. I believe, at that time, I may have been the only female over the age of fifty on a prime-time newscast.

At this point, I was also pretty certain any wish or dream I had of getting to the network was probably not going to happen, but there was also a graceful acceptance about that. Once again, I instinctively knew, there was something more I was supposed to do, although I had no clue what that was. But going to the network wasn't it.

As much as I loved the work, the storytelling, I knew I needed to begin to think about what I might do next. Something had to change.

One of my mentors suggested I make a list of at least five to ten people whom I admired in this community, people I could trust to go to for advice about what else I might do should I ever consider leaving television.

So, for two years, I went back to doing those informational interviews that got me my job in TV in the first place. I quietly and confidentially asked people I respected, "What does somebody like me do when you think—know—it's time to consider doing something else?" "What do you see me doing besides television?"

The reactions and answers were quite interesting. Some weren't really sure exactly what I did other than they watched me every night and they saw me "read the news." Trust me! It's a lot more than just that! They always asked me what I wanted to do or liked to do. Again, I had no clue how to answer those questions.

All I did know was that I somehow wanted to use all my experience and the skills I had honed over my entire life and the talents and gifts I believe I was blessed with at birth. I wanted to share all that knowledge with the hope of helping, inspiring, and motivating others, and yes, to also have a bit more control over my life.

Many made suggestions or offered ideas, but none of them quite got it, nor was it their fault. I began to realize that we were speaking two different languages. I had to figure out how to translate what I did in television—my actual skills—to something they could relate to, something they could understand in the corporate world. I had to use their language. For example: A project manager in the corporate world is very much like a producer/reporter in TV. One oversees the entire story from start to finish. The producer/reporter brings all the elements together. Or, in the corporate world, crisis management is similar to breaking news in television. Once I began to speak their language, not only did they begin to think differently about my skills and what my talents were, I began to own them as well.

There were many conversations with many people, and I hoped they were all confidential, but I have to wonder.

One day, I was asked by management, "Are you happy here?" It felt like a loaded question, and I chose my words very carefully. I answered by saying there was a sense of pride at the exclusive stories I had done over many years. I enjoyed the work of sharing important information with viewers, especially during turbulent, challenging times such as 9-11 or the Boston Marathon bombings. Those were the things that made me "happy." The topic never came up again, but I knew: it was time.

After much soul searching and countless meetings with people in the corporate world, I narrowed it down to three possible paths.

I could maybe be a communications expert at some big company but had no idea what company would want me. (*Who would want me with no corporate experience?)* I could maybe be an executive director of a nonprofit organization, even though I had never been one. Or… I could start my own business.

When I shared this three-lane approach with one of my mentors, he emphatically said to me, "Liz! You're well-known, you're well-respected, you have credibility. **That** is value. **Why** would you give **that** value to someone else? Start your business, and if in six months or nine months you don't have any clients, or you don't like what you're doing, **then** you can always go and do something else."

It was as if a kaleidoscope went click. Suddenly, in an instant, everything came into focus. I knew that's what I would do. I could help people with presence, public speaking, storytelling, messaging, and so much more. How could I *not* see it when it was right in front of me?! Even executive coaches need their own "coach" from time to time.

But, now what? How do I do this? *How* do I start a business? I'd never wanted to have my own business, and I never thought I was smart enough to run one. That was a limiting belief! (More on that subject coming up in Chapter Four.) *God forbid, what if I failed? What if I had no clients?* I was petrified! Was I really doing the right thing? Was this what I was supposed to do next?

Fear isn't a good enough reason to stop.

And yet, there was something so deep within me urging me on. I kept coming back to one of my favorite quotes from Dr. Robert Schuller,

"What would you attempt to do if you knew you could not fail?" To me, if fear was the only thing stopping me, that simply was not a good enough reason.

Although the decision to leave WCVB had been made, at my request, it was not public knowledge for a couple of months. I needed time to prepare, in private. While secretly cleaning off the shelves in my office one night, some of my doubt—but not all of it—dissipated when I found a résumé tape from a woman who was currently a reporter at Channel 5. However, she had sent me that tape, requesting I review it, long before getting to WCVB. Her questions included: What did she need to do to get better? What did she need to do to get into this top ten market? She was from the Boston area, currently working in a Florida TV station, and wanted very much to come back home.

I'd forgotten all about that tape, or that I even still had it, along with my three-page, single-spaced critique/feedback I had written and sent to her. As I looked over my copy of that long letter I had sent her, I had a moment of clarity: I'd already been doing this kind of work.

For years, I willingly gave my help and gladly shared my expertise with those brave enough to ask. Young reporters shared their reels, looking to improve their on-camera performance and storytelling, and interns asked for my help in shoring up their own direction. They were asking *me* for advice, for professional coaching. I realized that my own experience, approachability, personality, and skills were enough to launch into the next chapter of my life. Yes, I was doing the right thing. I had been doing it for years! I left Channel 5, launched my business, and never looked back. I jumped off the cliff!

There was so much to learn! When I began my business, I honestly felt like I knew nothing. I'd been told I needed to put a business plan together, but I had no idea how or what exactly that meant! How would I get clients? Would anyone want to work with me? I had no track record to prove I could do what I was setting out to do. How much do I charge if I even get any clients at all? Where could I even go to find out what other coaches' fees were? Most do not post any of that information on their websites. Bottom line: How in the world do I build a business?

Thankfully, I once again allowed myself to be authentic and vulnerable with the right people and asked a lot of the right questions. To my surprise, many were very willing to help me figure it out, but I also began to own more of me. I realized I knew more than I thought I did. I had more skills than I even realized I had. I just had to use them in a different and new way. No knowledge is ever wasted. Did I have to learn a lot of new things? Absolutely, but that's okay. I began to trust myself enough to say, "I will figure this out."

I did get clients quickly too. In fact, my first client session was in New York City the day after I signed off the air. Other clients and engagements followed shortly thereafter.

One of them was from a local company, who wanted to hire me to host the launch of their new real estate properties. When they inquired about my fee, I wasn't even sure I knew what to suggest it would be. After much thinking, I did throw out a number for this event, and lo and behold, it was exactly what they were planning to offer me, and it was a nice chunk of change! I was thrilled!

In the past, when I did any speaking or hosting, I was not contractually allowed to accept any fees while working on TV. The few times that organizations may have insisted on compensating me, I donated that money to a favorite charity.

There was even one occasion where my donation ended up buying a whole new set of uniforms for a local high school basketball team. No one but the coach and a small handful of people knew where the money had come from for those spiffy new jerseys, but I was very proud that I was able to do that for them, all because someone felt I, and my time, were valuable enough to pay me for it.

I'm a risk-taker or, as I like to say, a calculated, intelligent risk-taker. I left teaching without knowing what I would do next, got into television with no real experience, and yes, I became an award-winning journalist after twenty-eight years in the industry, even without wearing the "Big J" on my chest, and I took a risk to launch a business in my 50s! Believe me, I know how lucky I am. I had a very public platform from which to launch, and not everyone has that. While that may have helped me get started, it's been determination, persistence, perseverance, hard work, resilience, and drive that has helped me grow my company into a thriving endeavor.

Every experience I have ever had through childhood, along with every job I ever held, have all contributed to my growth. No knowledge is ever wasted.

Now, as an executive communications coach, I am a teacher once again, coming full circle.

I am blessed to have the opportunity to share all my experiences, expertise, and insights with clients around the world: to help them find their own voice, to own who they are, to dream and create their next chapter, and to live their best life.

Sometimes, creating that next chapter involves taking risks.

What would any of us do if we took more risks? If we knew we wouldn't fail? How many dreams get pushed aside because of fear? Or because we stay stuck, paralyzed to make a move one way or another? Or because it's too scary to be our authentic self and own who we are at a soul level? Yes, it may feel like jumping off a cliff, but I'm so glad I did. I created my next chapter.

Time To Reflect:

Ask yourself: what's the biggest risk you've taken, both personally and/or professionally? What opportunity did I let slip by out of fear? What dreams do I still have that I've put on a back burner for whatever rational—and perhaps irrational—reasons I may have? What would I attempt to do if I knew I wouldn't fail?

Whatever your answers to any of those questions are, can you do anything differently? Are you brave enough to revisit those dreams? Make today the day you make the decision to take a risk, conquer a fear, or step out of your comfort zone. I can promise you, if you do, you will transform your life!

2

Accepting and Celebrating Our True Selves

If we are filled with self-doubt, we become our own worst enemy!

~ Liz Brunner

I'm a Mosaic

Everyone's family is unique. But have you ever thought about how your family shaped who you are? Culture, traditions, and family stories combine to form our identity, actions, and beliefs about ourselves. I'm proud of my family tree and my generational roots, which have impacted my life in profound and sometimes unexpected ways.

At my first television station in Champaign-Urbana, Illinois, I hadn't been on the air long when the question of my ethnicity began to surface. As I went bounding up to the lobby's reception desk one day, our vice president happened to be standing there and turned to me and said, “Well, let’s just ask her.”

“Ask me what?” I replied.

“We have a caller on the line who wants to know if you are black or white. What do you want us to tell them?”

“Seriously?”

“Yes. What would you like us to tell them?”

Quite stunned, I paused and then said, “Tell them I’m an American!”

This was not the first time, nor would it be the last, that my ethnicity or nationality would be a topic of discussion.

Although I was born in Connecticut, we moved to Hawaii when I was only a year old. As a young child, growing up in the islands, playing on the beach with my three younger brothers, my mom was often asked by the *haoles* (pronounced “howlies,” aka tourists), “Oh! Can we take a picture of your beautiful Hawaiian family*?”* That question happened so many times that my mom gave up trying to tell them that we didn’t have a drop of Hawaiian blood in us. We were dark-skinned, not only because of her Indian background but also because we spent a lot of time in the bright Hawaiian sun.

One of the things I treasure most about growing up in the islands is that we lived among various nationalities: Hawaiian, Japanese, Chinese, Filipino, African American, and so many more.

By the age of ten, we'd moved to "lily white" Pekin, Illinois, where it was known that the KKK was quite active. Our high school sports teams were named the Pekin Chinks. Supposedly, the pervading myth was that if you drilled straight down through the earth from Pekin, Illinois, you would come out in Peking, China. I have no idea if that is true! The school team and mascot have since been changed to the Dragons.

Think back to when you were ten years old. If you had lived in the same town all your life at that point, you probably had your own circle of friends, felt a sense of belonging, of being included.

Now, imagine moving to a new town, in the middle of fourth grade, where everyone had their established cliques. I felt so different from everyone else in my new hometown. Nobody looked like me.

My skin was very dark. I had long, brown, wavy hair. I always felt like an outsider. While I am predominantly Indian, one-fourth to be specific, I am a mosaic of nationalities: Indian, Spanish, German, French, Dutch, even a little Scottish, supposedly a descendant of Mary, Queen of Scots.

Moving to Illinois was probably the first time I began to feel prejudice. I was teased and taunted and called a "Hawaiian nigger." My eldest brother was also called that derogatory term by his own football coach. I used to go home crying, not understanding why they were calling me this name, or what it meant. My brother and I were both confused.

But it wasn't only at school that I felt the glares. My father, Rev. Galen E. Russell, Jr., was senior pastor of our church, and when my godmother, Dr. Abbie Clement Jackson, came to visit, the energy in the sanctuary changed. Aunt Abbie was a very smart, proud African American woman whom I adored. Her own mother, Emma C. Clement, became the first African American woman to be named American Mother of the Year by The Golden Rule Foundation in 1946. The Golden Rule Foundation was founded by Eleanor Roosevelt, Mamie Eisenhower, JC Penney, and Norman Vincent Peale to recognize women who provided inspiration and instruction to the nation's future.

Parishioners were polite and respectful to Aunt Abbie because my dad was senior pastor and I was his daughter, but many didn't know how to behave nor what to say.

Having been born and raised in India, my mom was always very sensitive about both the color of her skin and of a culture historically demeaning to women.

At the age of eighteen, she crossed the ocean, moving to America to attend Oberlin College and then on to Case Western Reserve to pursue her master's in social work. In those days, that was quite rare.

Being half-Indian and half-white, and in the United States, she was always keenly aware of how being a woman with dark-brown skin was fodder for prejudice, discrimination, and racism. But her parents too faced their own challenges because of their nationalities.

Her father, my grandfather, Dr. C. Joseph Chacko, a professor of international law and political science, was 100 percent Indian, born and raised. His ancestry can be traced back to the old Chaldean Syrian Church, which was established by the apostle St. Thomas in southwest India in 52 AD when twelve Indian families were converted to Christianity.

My grandmother, Dr. Dorothy Dunning Chacko, was about as New England as you can get. Although Grandmother Chacko was born in Japan, she was raised in Massachusetts and is a descendent of William Brewster, who came over on the Mayflower, December 22, 1620 (Dunning 2011). Other descendants arrived in Boston in 1638 when this pioneer town was only eight years old with a population of one thousand people. Family lore says those ancestors also owned the land that is now the Boston Common when it was a cow pasture. Maybe that's one of the reasons I felt so drawn to Boston.

Graduating at the top of her class at Smith College in 1925, Grandmother Chacko went on to receive her medical degree from Columbia University's College of Physicians and Surgeons and completed additional training at The School of Tropical Medicine in England. She was also the first female resident in medicine, and then in surgery, at New York's Metropolitan Hospital.

She and my grandfather met while they were both attending Columbia University, but knowing that if they married, they would each face some life-altering paths, they spent four years praying about whether it was wise to marry or not. A white woman marrying an Indian man in the 1930s was practically unheard of! "An American woman who married an 'ineligible alien' (Indian, Chinese, or Japanese man) lost her citizenship," said my grandmother.

She automatically became a citizen of India, but marriage to my white grandmother meant my grandfather would not be allowed to become his church's first Indian bishop. He would remain a deacon.

They moved to India in 1932. Grandfather was the president of St. Andrew's College. Grandmother was a doctor at two colleges, and with her specialty being tropical diseases, worked in village clinics, earning acceptance by the Indian people. In 1964, she also founded Bethany Village in the region of Punjab, which was the first treatment and rehabilitation colony for those suffering from leprosy.

In 1967, my grandparents moved to Pennsylvania. Grandfather Chacko was a professor at Widener College. Grandmother was working at Crozer-Chester Medical Center. Along with her medical duties, she was also president of the Chester, Pennsylvania, YWCA from 1974-1976, a community that was extremely segregated in the 70s.

She was SO determined to fight racism and bring people together that, despite my grandfather's strong objections and fears for her safety, she "dared" to organize a luau, bringing the YWCA and the YMCA together. She would not be deterred.

The other side of my family tree, my dad's side, was equally as strong in promoting cultural diversity. My grandpa, Rev. Galen E. Russell, Sr., and Grammie, Beatrice Price Russell, lived in Japan for many years, ministering and teaching conversational English. My two sets of grandparents were friends from their church work. It was in Japan that my parents first met. My mom was on a French freighter with her mother, traveling to America to go to Oberlin. Japan happened to be one of the stops on their leg to the U.S. Yup! They were the only two women on board with that shipload of French sailors. It was the cheapest way to get to the U.S. Grandmother always said she was there to chaperone.

My father was engaged to someone else when he met my mom in Japan, and it was years later before they met once again as camp counselors at Lake Winnipesaukee in New Hampshire! *I know, crazy!* Obviously, he never married the other woman.

Grammie was educated at New York University, Columbia University, and Union Theological Seminary. Again, this was a time when many women were not going to college, let alone *allowed* to do so in some cases. She was so supportive of young girls that she devoted more than seventy-five consecutive years to the Girl Scouts of America, including organizing the first troop in Harlem.

Everywhere Grammie traveled in the world, she preached diversity and women's empowerment, spiritually adopting as many young people with different cultural backgrounds as she could. It was her way of having this truly "international family." Dinners at her home looked like the U.N.!

When I arrived in Tampa, Florida, the second stop on my television career tour, I felt a bit more accepted because it was a very transient community. Many people who lived there had moved from someplace else to find lower taxes, better weather, and lots of sunshine.

The city pulsed with people of all nationalities, and many ethnic groups claimed me as one of their own. The Cubans thought I was Cuban; the Hispanics thought I was one of them; even the African Americans saw my dark brown, very curly, permed hair and thought I must be Black. It also didn't hurt that I used to jokingly say I could get a tan just taking the garbage out. Thanks, Mom, for my olive complexion. (My dermatologist would be happy to know I now wear sunscreen!)

Being considered ethnic didn't hurt my career either given many television stations were trying to be more diverse. If I had known back then what I now know today about the TV business, I might have seriously considered changing my last name to my mother's maiden name of Chacko. I could have legitimately, and maybe should have, checked off the minority box. I often wonder what impact that could have had on my career.

Moving to Boston, my third television stop, was the exact opposite of Tampa in many ways. Families had been there for generation upon generation. They were well established, and even though my roots on my maternal grandmother's side were clearly very New England, my family was spread out all around the world. Once again, I felt like an outsider.

I had my big, curly Miss America hair and was also very tan from my five years of living in the Florida sunshine. No one really seemed to know what my nationality was.

While I believe, still to this day, that I was hired for my skills, a couple of years into my tenure at WCVB-Boston, I learned of a rumor that was circulating that management thought they had hired a "light-skinned black woman." Now, I did replace an African American woman who left, but was the rumor true? I have no idea, nor have I ever felt the need to validate it.

I was once up for a network job at ABC-TV in New York. My competition: an African American woman and a Hispanic woman, who eventually got the job.

I was a prisoner locked inside unconscious expectation.

I'm not here to say that my experiences were horrible, or traumatic, or could possibly compare to what others endured before me, nor what any of you may have been through in your own journey through this lifetime, but this is my heritage.

I am a melting pot. I am a mosaic. I am an American.

Who I am is because of where I've been and those who came before me. I own all of that, and I'm also proud of it too.

But it also impacted me in surprising ways that I am only now discovering. In revisiting my family history for this book, I had a profound revelation of why I felt compelled to share the story of my ancestors. It's not simply the experiences of prejudice that they or I faced, but more importantly, the weight of this heritage that I have felt and carried with me and how that has played into my own confidence issues, both professionally and personally. I became, at times, a prisoner of my own making, locked inside this unconscious expectation I felt I had to live up to, this lineage of ancestors who had accomplished so much. I believe it's one of the reasons I have strived so hard in every area of my life, all the time!

Even my own mother admitted to me she too has felt the burden. It's one of the reasons she chose not to go to her mother's alma mater of Smith College, so as not to be constantly asked if she was Dr. Dorothy Dunning's daughter.

Expectations. We put them on ourselves unknowingly. They may also be overt because a parent wants us to follow in their footsteps to become a lawyer or a doctor when our heart is elsewhere. All of it impacts one's confidence. And when it does, we often feel alone on our own island.

Outsider Syndrome

My nationality wasn't the only thing that made me feel like an outsider. Growing up, I never felt accepted, or fit in, whatever "fitting in" means! I wasn't one of the popular kids. I didn't hang out with the smart kids, or the athletes and cheerleaders. Honestly, I don't know who I hung out with. Music and drama were my interests, but I don't think I hung out with those kids much either. Sure, I was friendly with a lot of people, but I had very few true friends, let alone anyone I would call my best friend. Outsider. That was me.

Growing up, I had dolls I played with, but having a Barbie doll? Out of the question! Too superficial.

I never felt like one of the pretty girls. My long, wavy brown hair was parted down the middle, like all the other girls, but they all had straight, shiny hair and always looked beautiful to me. How I wished my hair was straight.

Wearing makeup was forbidden until I was sixteen years old, and even then, it was minimal and only for special occasions. I don't recall what qualified as a "special occasion," but it was rare. I was envious of my classmates who got to wear makeup.

I had thick Coke-bottle glasses. I desperately wanted contact lenses, but if I was ever going to get them, I would have to pay for them myself. It was not a luxury my family could afford. It wasn't until my sophomore year in high school that I'd saved up enough babysitting money that I finally bought my contact lenses.

I wouldn't call myself necessarily fat. I considered myself pudgy until about age seventeen.

Add to that the culture shock I felt and feelings of being an outsider when we moved from Hawaii to Illinois in the middle of the fourth grade.

Yet, these are some of the experiences that filled me with much self-doubt and rejection. In hindsight, I realize a lot of this had to do with my own lack of self-confidence, but it also had to do with other girls, women—other than my own mother— who rarely, if ever, were supportive in any way.

During my junior year while studying music at Lawrence University in Appleton, Wisconsin, I was competing for Miss Illinois 1979. I won the title, which put me into the Miss America Pageant. The Miss America Pageant system is a scholarship competition, and contestants must have a talent to enter. Mine was singing. I'm proud to say that because of participating in the program, I paid every penny of my college education.

Typically, my schedule during my reign was attending classes Monday through Wednesday, leaving Appleton on Thursday, driving south to fulfill my appearance schedule in Illinois over the weekend, and turning right around on Sunday, driving back to school. There were some days those car trips were twelve hours long, or more. It was exhausting, but it was my job.

Upon returning to Appleton from one of my road trips, my dorm hallway's full-length mirror was off the wall. Where did I find it? In my room, with a note that read: "Now you can look at yourself all day long." I was devastated. How could they be so cruel, and why? Was it jealousy? Of what exactly I don't know. All it did was fill me with more self-doubt as I struggled with feelings of not being accepted by other women.

Many more unkind experiences would cause me to freeze in my tracks as I navigated my professional life. Oftentimes, women were the worst offenders. Whether it was a fellow female anchor who was so afraid I would take her job that instead of helping me be successful for the greater good of the broadcast, it felt like she did many things to sabotage me, or a producer who threw me under the bus for a mistake ***she*** made when approving a story I wrote.

She didn't take responsibility for her actions out of fear the news director would have a negative opinion of her managerial skills. *Why couldn't we all just lift each other up?*

That same female news director sent me on a last-minute out-of-state political assignment, which I felt was surely some test of whether I had what it took to be in that business. I was determined. There was NO way I was going to fail, and I didn't. Did she ever say "Good job"? Hell no!

Perhaps one of the most shocking offenses occurred early into my new business. A female CEO of a huge firm in Boston—who prided herself on being supportive of other women and had told me so on several occasions—introduced me to a male CEO of another company: "Meet Liz Brunner. You should see her in Flywheel. She has one of the best bodies in Boston!" (Flywheel was an indoor cycling class.) I was mortified and thought it horribly inappropriate! How would this man ever take me seriously or hire me as an executive coach to work with his team?

When I first moved to Boston to take on the role of correspondent and fill-in anchor for the nightly news magazine show *Chronicle*, I neither spoke of being Miss Illinois nor that I'd competed in the Miss America Pageant. Back in 1993, Boston was still very conservative and provincial in some ways. As a result, I worried that the audience and my colleagues at the television station wouldn't take me seriously, that I might be perceived as being superficial because I competed in a so-called beauty pageant. But the biggest reason I didn't talk about it was because—right or wrong—I was too afraid it would be just one more thing women would hold against me.

Oddly enough, this was one of the reasons I often went into work daily without ANY makeup on; I intentionally tried to downplay my looks. Perhaps the perception by some was that I was lazy or didn't care, but it was more than that. I hoped they would see the real me. Instead, I got remarks like, "I hate you. You look so good without any makeup on!" How do you respond to that? I've never considered myself beautiful. My thought was, *Okay, I guess I'm a little better-looking than the average bear, but beautiful? Not so much.* More self-doubt? Perhaps. My standard reply when people offered up a compliment was to add humor and simply say, "I chose my grandparents very carefully."

My appearance, no doubt, has served me well, particularly in an industry where looks matter as much as they do, and I am grateful that I learned how to dress, how to apply makeup, etc., but I'm still me. I'm still Liz, the woman who had to learn to let go of all those fears and negative voices playing in her head since childhood. I had to learn to get out of my own way.

The most important story is the one we tell ourselves.

To this day, my appearance is still fodder for a comment. In an introductory phone call with a new client, she emphatically told me she doesn't wear makeup, or do her nails, or wear high heels. Imagine my surprise when this highly successful C-suite executive arrived for our first session wearing heels, makeup, and having her nails beautifully manicured. She went on to say that she knows her appearance matters, and she wants to do something about it, but then, in an authentic and deeply vulnerable voice, followed it up with, “I don’t look like you.” Talk about wearing your heart on your sleeve. Her own feelings of self-doubt suddenly rose to the surface.

How often do so many of us judge ourselves by what we think we are not?

In the wise and widely used words of Brenè Brown: “Because true belonging only happens when we present our authentic, imperfect selves to the world, our sense of belonging can never be greater than our level of self-acceptance.”

Our desire for approval and acceptance is real, it is human nature, and while we may desire that from the outside world, it’s more important to accept ourselves for who we are on the inside.

Imposter Syndrome

Have you ever felt like a fraud? As if you are not qualified for the success you have or not good enough to be doing what you are doing or being where you are? That somehow you will be found out? Maybe you even question if you are deserving of any of the accolades you are receiving.

You are filled with self-doubt.

That is often called “imposter syndrome” and an estimated 70 percent of people experience imposter feelings at some point in their lives (Craig 2018). I certainly have felt this way, more times than I care to count.

The term *imposter phenomenon*, more commonly called imposter syndrome, was coined in 1978 by two American psychologists, Pauline Clance and Suzanne Imes. It affects all kinds of people in all walks of life, and contrary to popular belief, these feelings are not a "female thing." Research has found that imposter syndrome affects men and women equally; however, it may manifest quite differently.

While women may be more vocal about it, men may suffer in silence because they are too ashamed to talk about it. One reason is societal expectations. From the time young boys are growing up, many are taught to save face, deny their problems, avoid their feelings, and certainly not talk about them. Even some of the most successful men can struggle with feelings of self-doubt, and yet, they are often afraid to admit it. That doesn't allow for vulnerability.

Sometimes childhood traumas play a role in why even a very successful person experiences imposter syndrome, as was the case for former Navy SEAL Mark Divine.

Here's a guy who, at twenty-six-years-old, left a highly successful job on Wall Street as a CPA and joined the SEALS. There were 180 in his class, but only 19 successfully completed the rigorous training. Divine graduated top of his class.

Divine remained on active duty for nine years, eleven more on reserve. His mental and physical toughness, strength, and endurance set him apart early on in this elite group. His leadership was so effective that he went on to create SEAL training programs for the government.

Today, as the founder of SEALFIT and the Unbeatable Mind Academy, Mark is taking all his life experiences, philosophies, and SEAL training methods and teaching everyday citizens how to live their best lives. He is also an author of several books, including *Staring Down the Wolf: 7 Leadership Commitments that Forge Elite Teams* (2020), and *Unbeatable Mind: Forge Resiliency and Mental Toughness to Succeed at an Elite Level* (2014).

And yet, even with *all* of that success, Mark shared with me during his guest appearance on my podcast his feelings of insecurity at times.

"I have a little imposter syndrome... I grew up in a pretty rough family. There was a lot of alcohol and a lot of anger from my father and codependence on my mom's side. And so, like a lot of people, I didn't escape trauma… part of that trauma led me to have self-worth issues. So, no matter how successful I have become, I can tell you, Liz, that I've probably held myself back from 90 percent of my potential as a result of that. And so, I continue to work on that." (*Live Your Best Life with Liz Brunner.* 2021)

Feelings of self-doubt left another one of my podcast guests with such anxiety that it led to nearly debilitating panic attacks. Petra Kolber was an internationally renowned fitness expert, noted in *The New York Times* as one of the most likely to succeed, and was even on the back of a Kellogg's Special K cereal box. To the outside world, she was living this amazing life, and yet, even though she was enjoying many aspects of her fame, on the inside she was suffering from serious feelings of self-doubt. Petra believes, like Mark, that much of it stemmed from her childhood. Growing up just outside of Liverpool, England, she said it was almost frowned upon if you stood out in any way. Add to that an old tape that kept playing in her head from some of her coaches telling her, "You're never going to make it."

"I felt like that imposter. Who am I really to be deserving of this success? I wasn't taught to dream big. I was never smart enough. I was never good enough. It was a whole sense of 'This is so amazing, but I'm going to get found out, because who am **I** to be deserving of a life like that?'" (Brunner 2020)

Petra is a two-time cancer survivor and spent years dissolving many of those inner negative thoughts and limiting beliefs. In her book *The Perfection Detox: Tame Your Inner Critic, Live Bravely and Unleash Your Joy* she describes herself as a "recovering perfectionist" (2018).

While all of one's fears and anxieties may never fully disappear, Petra believes, and I concur, the most important story we will **ever** tell is the one we tell ourselves. We must get out of our own way and stop telling ourselves stories that aren't true.

...if we are filled with self-doubt, we become our own worst enemy!

I often remind clients, and myself, that if we are filled with self-doubt, we become our own worst enemy. We must learn to silence the inner critic.

Some researchers believe there are five types of imposter syndrome:

1) The Perfectionist: If every *t* is not crossed and every *i* not dotted, they feel they have failed in some way.
2) The Expert: They feel they should always be learning more about anything and everything. It's never enough.
3) The Natural Genius: If they struggle with learning something new, they feel they are failing because they expect themselves to "know it all" and for the process to be easy.
4) The Soloist: If they are praised for doing something for which they received assistance, they feel they don't deserve the credit.
5) The Superhuman: They must excel at everything they do or else it doesn't count. They are often workaholics (Neilson 2021).

Do you recognize yourself in any of those descriptions? Google searches yield a number of people who say they relate to or identify with the term *imposter syndrome*.

Michelle Obama, former First Lady: "I still have a little impostor syndrome… It doesn't go away, that feeling that you shouldn't take me that seriously. What do I know? I share that with you because we all have doubts in our abilities…"

Sheryl Sandberg, the COO of Facebook and founder of Lean In: "Every time I was called on in class, I was sure that I was about to embarrass myself. Every time I took a test, I was sure that it had gone badly. And every time I didn't embarrass myself—or even excelled—I believed that I had fooled everyone yet again. One day soon, the jig would be up."

Matt Higgins, entrepreneur and *Shark Tank* judge, comparing himself to fellow judges Mark Cuban and Kevin O'Leary: "You don't belong here, this is completely nuts, you're an imposter."

Albert Einstein, Nobel Prize Winner: "The exaggerated esteem in which my lifework is held makes me very ill at ease. I feel compelled to think of myself as an involuntary swindler."

Actor Don Cheadle: "All I can see is everything I'm doing wrong that is a sham and a fraud."

Academy Award-winning actor Tom Hanks: "There comes a point where you think, 'How did I get here?' When are they going to discover that I am, in fact, a fraud and take everything away from me?'"

Poet laureate Maya Angelou: "I have written eleven books, but each time, I think, 'Oh oh, they're going to find out now. I've run a game on everybody and they're going to find me out.'"

That is exactly how I felt when I landed my job as the director of community relations at WTVT-13, my second job in television. I was the only female in upper management, and I remember thinking, *They're going to find out that I've never been a manager before and I have NO idea how to do this job that didn't exist before I got here*! Yet again, a position was created, and I filled it, just as I had at my first TV station. Once again, I had to go back to the notion that just because I haven't done something doesn't mean I can't. I just have to try.

I really didn't know who I could possibly go to with questions. I didn't know who I could possibly be vulnerable and authentic with out of fear that I would be found out, discovered to be a fraud. I felt very alone in my learning-curve journey. Most of the time, I just kept my questions to myself and tried to figure things out on my own. I also did a lot of listening. I certainly didn't have any female role models I could turn to.

It wasn't long before my boss added yet another job to my responsibilities. I became the early morning news co-anchor. Yes, I was doing both jobs, working about eighty hours a week. Again, I'd never been a news anchor before. *How do I do this?* I was too afraid to ask anyone for advice, let alone tell them that I felt like I didn't know what the hell I was doing! I just tried to do my best.

One day, at the last minute, I was asked to be the fill-in host for our midday talk show, *Tampa Bay's Talking*. Besides being a live, thirty-minute talk show with a guest I would interview, there was a studio audience and viewers calling in with their questions and comments. Just before walking into the studio to meet the audience and the guest, my nerves were in high gear! I felt like an imposter. I'd never hosted a live talk show before! Sure, I had done a three-minute recorded show at WCIA in IL, but a live show, with an audience, and call-in questions. *OMG! What if I am horrible? What if I am a total flop?*

As I made my way to the set, I thought, *I have two options here. One, I could walk in and act all confident, as if I've done this many times before and know exactly what I am doing, or two, I could be honest with the audience and tell them the truth.* For whatever reason, I chose option two.

They greeted me with such enthusiasm and applause, and then I told them I'd never done this before, that I was scared, and then I asked them for their help. I was authentic; I was vulnerable. They were unbelievably supportive. They accepted me and applauded even more loudly than before the show had started.

Acceptance. We all want it. It's not only a normal part of the human condition, but also a fundamental need we all have: to feel accepted, to feel like we belong. It is rooted in our evolutionary history, says C. Nathan DeWall, PhD, a psychologist at the University of Kentucky.

When we don't feel like we are being accepted, it feels like rejection, and rejection hurts. As we move through life, it's inevitable that at some point, we will all face feelings of rejection, of not being accepted. For some, those feelings may have a long-lasting effect.

And while imposter syndrome is an inner feeling of self-doubt, outsider syndrome is all about feelings of acceptance. There is a subtle difference between the two, but both are limiting beliefs and often coexist and overlap.

Time To Reflect:

Whether it's imposter syndrome or outsider syndrome, none of us are alone when it comes to these feelings, and if they are severe or debilitating, we must all consider getting professional help.

Whenever you feel imposter syndrome or outsider syndrome rearing its head, think of some of the successes you have had. You may want to start to document some of those successes in a journal so that when you do feel those negative feelings coming on, you can refer to the wins in your life.

You may also consider documenting when those imposter or outsider feelings arise. Your feelings are never right or wrong, they are simply your feelings, but see if you can figure out why they are there and where they are coming from.

Is it a new job? Are you comparing yourself to others when it's not appropriate? Is it the need to be perfect? Is there a trigger and a pattern that you recognize? That's one way of figuring out if that inner critic has a point or it's just an old, negative tape playing in your head. Try to reframe the thought. This is about separating feelings from facts. Be conscious of the script that's in your head.

Accept that no one is perfect! Self-doubt can at times be paralyzing, but you can take steps to move forward and not get stuck.

3

The Power of Authenticity

Empowered women empower women.

~ Anonymous

Find Your Community

It's taken me nearly all my adult life to come to understand and accept that if we are filled with self-doubt, we become our own worst enemy! And many women—not all, but many—make it harder for us to put those negative thoughts out of our heads and take the risk of asking for help from anyone, especially another woman.

I think many of us want to be seen as strong, independent, and self-sufficient, and there is nothing wrong with that. I do too, but often we can't get to where we want to go without the help of others, and women need to help other women! We need to empower other women. We need to have our community of supporters. Yet, I'm convinced sometimes getting support from other women is harder than getting support from a man! This may be one of the biggest obstacles we face. Why is that?

My theory: Women sometimes feel threatened by other women for whatever reason, whether it's status, looks, or even the job they're trying to hold onto.

A young woman I know who was working at a national sports network learned that one of their major shows had an opening for assistant director (AD). No one had recommended her, but she was confident she could do the job. With courage, she approached the director of the show, who happened to be a woman. That director told her she was thrilled this young woman had reached out, and yes, the job was hers. The director also told her that she liked the idea of replacing the departing female AD with another woman.

Being a director of a show is a pretty big deal in the TV industry. And while more women are getting into the profession, and into that role, it's still a man's world. There are very few women who hold the title of director, let alone on a major, live national sports television broadcast.

The director orchestrates what the viewer sees at home. They handle everything from picking the camera shots, making the split-second decisions to capture the right reactions, to creating the look and feel of the show from start to finish. A good director is able to find the right balance between the adrenaline rush and frenetic energy of a control room during a live broadcast and can create calm in the midst of what often looks and feels like chaos. A director also needs a really good AD by his or her side.

This young woman who got the AD job knew she had a lot to learn, was more than willing to do so, and was thrilled to be growing

and contributing. Throughout the season of the show, she was told over and over again by colleagues how good she was, that she fit right in. They were all impressed with her work ethic and her ideas. Many even called her a "rock star." All except for one—the female director.
At the end of the show's season, this young woman got called into her boss's office and was told she was not going to be on the show anymore. She was being fired.

Confused by the sudden turn around, she wanted to know why. All she was told was it was the director's decision. So, once again finding courage, she reached out to the director and simply asked what she had done wrong. What could she have done differently? The answer she got: "I think you want to direct this show, and I'm not letting that happen."

Not once did this young woman express an interest in directing, and yet she was being thrown off the show because her female director felt threatened. And the irony in this story is that this same director told a national sports publication that she always had a hard time finding up-and-coming women to mentor. Talk about a missed opportunity.

We all have had feelings of insecurity, but that insecurity, fear, or jealousy not only hurts us as individuals, but it also holds all of us back as a collective group.

When women can speak authentically and honestly with other women, when we share our fears and our self-doubts, when we can be collaborative, we gain strength and power. We move forward by working WITH one another, not against.

If every woman is honest with herself, I believe that at least at one time in her life she has felt jealous, insecure, or intimidated by another woman.

I remember walking into a grand hotel in Florida for a large international women's conference at which I was asked to speak. Hundreds of high-profile women from around the world were in attendance. As I surveyed the room, I noticed all of them looking like they were dressed to the nines! Their hair was perfectly coiffed and nails perfectly manicured. Their designer shoes elegantly matched their designer attire. Every major fashion house was represented in handbags alone.

And I thought to myself, *What could I possibly tell this group of obviously highly successful, polished looking women about presence and brand?* Talk about feeling a bit intimidated!

I took a deep breath, rolled my shoulders back, and with every ounce of courage I could find, walked out onto that stage, determined to push aside any insecurities I had about the remarks I would share. I had to believe in myself. I had to own me.

I felt like I was taking down some veil of secrecy...

In the throes of launching my business, I consulted with many women and men. I had to be vulnerable enough to share my fears and self-doubts. I had to ask for help. Boy was that hard! I felt like I was taking down some veil of secrecy, that somehow these people

I was seeking advice from would look at me differently. No longer would they see me as this confident news anchor.

My courage to reach out came from reading best-selling author Keith Ferrazzi's book *Never Eat Alone* where he says, "Until you become as willing to ask for help as you are to give it… you are only working half the equation" (2014, 43). I didn't know a thing about being an entrepreneur, so unless I was willing to risk it and ask for help, I wasn't going to get very far.

I remember admitting that fear with one of my mentors who simply said, "You're smart. You'll figure it out!" Wow! That was powerful. Thankfully, I did—and still am figuring it out—but it was only because I risked asking for help. I risked being vulnerable and authentic.

The Courage to be Real

Being authentic and vulnerable does take courage, but it also requires a balance between the two. And there is a big difference between being authentic and emotional.

Authenticity allows for deeper connections and relationships while creating trust. It also demonstrates to the other person a level of confidence in oneself. Being too emotional, on the other hand, can completely dilute that perception.

That's one of the biggest mistakes people often make when attempting to show authenticity and vulnerability. They inadvertently show too much emotion or share too much personal information with strangers, which is not vulnerability. In fact, it might even be perceived as manipulation.

Vulnerability is sharing our feelings and experiences with people who have *earned* the right to hear them.

Oprah is a prime example of someone who is authentic and vulnerable. Love her or not, I believe she is someone who has found the balance between the two. I've been fortunate to meet and interview her over the years and have always had tremendous respect for her because of her ability to be both at the same time. During her daytime talk show's heyday, she had legions of fans with whom she had built up a trust, day in and day out. They had *earned* the right to hear her stories.

Once I was willing to be more vulnerable, many people became more willing to help me. So much so that I almost felt guilty of the support I was getting, that is until another one of my mentors said to me, "Liz, you were in our homes giving us the news, comforting us during troubled times. You've been in this community for twenty years, giving of your time, talent, and energy. You were building your business even before you started it." I'd never thought of it like that. Words like these allowed me to graciously accept all that was being offered.

Many people gave me great advice, and if I'm being totally honest, much of it came from men, who were more willing to help me than women. Yes, there were women who were in my corner, and I am so grateful for them, but it was the men who followed through on their support more often than the women.

None of us can go it alone. I believe for anyone, male or female, to be successful in the workplace and overcome professional obstacles, several roles should be filled: you need mentors, you need supporters, you need sponsors, you need to network. That is your community. And you need to be willing to ask for help. That is not an easy thing for most of us to do, especially women.

Since launching my business, I've been fortunate to work with many amazing people, both women and men, including C-suite executives, or those looking to get there, entrepreneurs, other journalists, and people who just want to continue to grow—to create their next chapter. And no matter how confident they portray themselves to be, the one thing many have in common is some feeling of self-doubt, which then leads to fears of being vulnerable enough to reveal one's authentic self.

And sometimes there's so much fear that people become paralyzed when it comes to being willing to be more authentic. I've had the opportunity to spend time with world-renowned executive leadership coach and author Marshall Goldsmith. Together with women's leadership expert Sally Helgesen, they coauthored a book: *How Women Rise.* In it they discuss how many women—and yes, I believe this applies to men too—fall into what they describe as the "superstition trap."

"I behave this way, I am successful—therefore I am successful because I behave this way" (2018, 4).

That is simply not an accurate way to assess one's success. Goldsmith and Helgesen suggest that as human beings, we are creatures of positive reinforcement. We tend to continue to repeat behaviors that have created success for us in the past, assuming that those actions will continue to work for us in the future. We have a belief, a superstition, a fear, that IF we make ANY changes to our habits or behaviors, we will not achieve that same success nor get that same positive reinforcement. As a result, we get stuck, even trapped, and sometimes it's those very behaviors—that we are unwilling to change—that can get in our way.

Yes, perhaps some people are successful because they do a lot of things right, even though some of what they do actually works against them, like withholding authenticity.

I can't tell you how many times I've heard clients tell me, "Well, I've always done 'it' this way," whatever IT is. "This is my authentic self, and I'm not going to change or try to do anything differently. That's just not me."

My response is this: If you are not getting the results you want, if you are not being seen and heard as you intend, then perhaps you need to understand and come to grips with the fact that a particular behavior or habit may not be working for you.

And, according to Goldsmith and Helgesen, if you persist in doing it YOUR way, that's not being authentic, it's just being stubborn, and you may need to question your motivation.

Simply put, you are not willing to make changes.

No doubt, change can be very difficult. Our brains like certainty. It's easier to stay in a "comfort zone" than venture into the unknown.

Change is about learning new skills, forming new habits, and maintaining them. It's one of the reasons, when I work with people, it's not just one session and then we're done. It takes time to learn new habits and release the old ones that we cling to. And often as the coach, I help keep people accountable, session after session. But for any change to occur and stick, one must be ready on an emotional level. Whether it's to lose weight, quit smoking, or yes, even be more authentic and vulnerable, change is a process, and it begins with taking responsibility for actions and behaviors.

"Each of us must take 100 percent responsibility for where we are in our life," says Jack Canfield. In his book *The Success Principles: How to Get from Where You are to Where You Want to Be,* taking responsibility is principle number one. It's the foundational principle and probably the hardest one to grasp too (2004).

Jack is also the co-creator of the *Chicken Soup for the Soul®* series of books, which have sold 500 million copies worldwide and have been translated into forty-three different languages. I interviewed Jack on my podcast, and we talked about his own personal next chapters from inner-city high school teacher to #1 *New York Times* best-selling author multiple times, to international motivational speaker and success coach.

He believes that we all must act as if we are 100 percent responsible for where our lives are. "You've either created it, promoted it or allowed it to be that way… when people act as if that's true… their lives dramatically change, they get healthier, they make more money, they have better relationships... the reality is when we act from that perspective, everything in life works better" (2021).

Taking responsibility is also about looking at oneself honestly and authentically. Being vulnerable with ourselves can be scary. I know it certainly has been for me at times. It can fill us with more self-doubt, which makes it even harder.

And yet, I now believe that all of us—at one time or another—are overcome with self-doubt, feel like an outsider, or have had our own imposter and outsider syndrome moments, or perhaps we are afraid to be authentic and vulnerable. Remember, research says at least 70 percent of us have those feelings at some point in time. Maybe it's simply human nature. We all want to be liked, accepted, included, and to feel that we matter!

During the 1985 Academy Awards show, Sally Fields's Oscar acceptance speech for the 1984 film *Places in the Heart* caused quite a stir. She ecstatically and tearfully proclaimed, "I can't deny the fact that you like me. Right now, you like me." Ms. Fields was ridiculed loudly for her authenticity and vulnerability.

Ms. Fields may have been publicly chastised for being so authentic, but I believe vulnerability is a risk worth taking. Be vulnerable with the right people. Ask for help from the right people. You just might be surprised at what will happen if you do.

Time To Reflect:

Women: Consider a time when you have been jealous, insecure, or even intimidated around another woman. How did you handle the situation? What were your words and your actions? What could you have done differently?

Men: Have you been as supportive of a colleague—male or female—as you could have been, or have you allowed your own fears to get in the way? Maybe you were worried about your job? What could you have done differently?

Can we all find more ways to be more encouraging, to listen more with intention?

If each of us can become a sponsor, supporter, or mentor to another human being, if we can let go of our own fears and self-doubt, imagine what could be accomplished! Be willing to take that chance. We all rise when we lift one another up.

4

The Courage of Confidence

Life begins at the end of your comfort zone.
~ Neale Donald Walsch

The Magic Ingredient

"Just be yourself, Liz," said the television consultant who was critiquing my on-air tapes and trying to help me become a better news anchor.

"But I am!" I loudly and defiantly proclaimed.

How wrong I was in my statement. It took nearly all my twenty-eight years of being on TV, and then leaving the industry, before I learned how to be more of me, more of my authentic self, to own who I am, to truly *feel* confident.

I'd like to think I portrayed confidence most of the time, but deep down inside, I wasn't always as confident as I would like to have been, an odd concept given my upbringing.

There was an unspoken expectation in my family that I could, or at least *should*, be able to easily get up in front of people and speak, sing, or act in a play with total confidence because that's what people did. That's what WE did.

But I didn't always have it all together, and still don't from time to time. Besides the childhood experiences of imposter and outsider syndrome I shared in Chapter Two, upon reflection, I think there was a perception by some that I *did* have it all together. That I was *always* confident.

That's a mistake many people often make. They assume a person is confident because they may make it look easy. However, we often neither know what's really going on in a person's life, nor what's inside their heart and mind. Assumptions are often not accurate.

Assumptions are also often made that if someone *appears* to be confident, that should equate to their level of competence. However, according to Professor Tomas Chamorro-Premuzic from University College London, that outward assumption of confidence may not be an accurate assessment of one's competence. He says in a podcast, "In virtually every culture, and especially the Western world, we tend to equate confidence with competence" (2014). The professor goes on to say that we automatically assume confident people are also more able, skilled, or talented.

When I was competing in the Miss America Pageant system, there may have been a perception or assumption that I was totally confident because, after all, I put myself into the competition in the first place. Yes, I believed I had what it took to win. I was competent in my talent, my skill as a singer, but as I looked around at the incredibly bright, talented, and beautiful group of women I was competing against, I wondered to myself: *Are they all as confident as they appear or want the rest of us to believe? Or do they, too, have moments of self-doubt?*

Little did I realize the pageant world would prepare me so well for the world of television, and later, my role as an executive communications coach. I understand what it *feels* like not to have the confidence you *wish* you had. It takes courage to be confident. It means getting out of your comfort zone, and to push yourself beyond your comfort zone also takes courage.

We live in a world that is very competitive. Whether in sports, school, or the workplace, competition exists on some level in every job. But let's be real, the TV business takes competition to a whole new level. There is almost always someone, somewhere who wants your job, or some consultant or TV executive who has an opinion of what you should look like, sound like, or who you should be. With that kind of constant scrutiny and competition, you'd better find a way to have confidence running through your veins.

I was convinced, at every TV station where I worked, all my colleagues were not only more confident than me, but also more competent and knowledgeable. After all, I didn't have a journalism or communications degree, whereas most of them did. I had so much to learn. To me, from the outside looking in, they all looked—or at least acted—like they had all the confidence in the world.

Factor in our uber hyped-up, social media world today, where everyone looks like they are on top of the world, living the dream, while showing their creative, fun, and successful lives. We even may begin to believe, consciously or unconsciously, that others are more confident or competent, but again, that is not reality.

It may be hard to sift through all the froth, but I think real, authentic confidence is still recognized, admired, and respected. It's also a reality that appearing more confident, especially at work, often leads to more promotions and opportunities.

We know what confident people look like, the advantages they have, and that is worth emulating. But how do we each master that on our own? What do we need to be doing to build up our own confidence?

If you look up the word *confidence* in any dictionary, it suggests something like this: a belief or trust in abilities, of oneself or one's powers, to act effectively. Simply put, confidence means you believe you can do something, while competence means you already have the ability to do it—that skill set. The relationship between the two means competence can lead to confidence, but not always.

To clarify even further, confidence and self-esteem are also not the same thing, although they are often linked. As suggested, confidence is the term we use to describe how we feel about our ability to perform roles, functions, and tasks, that belief. Self-esteem, on the other hand, is how we feel about *ourselves*.

My experiences interviewing and coaching people from all walks of life have convinced me that how we feel about ourselves, our self-esteem, has even more of an impact on our lives at times than our level of confidence.

I meet a lot of very confident, competent people, but it's interesting to notice that some don't always feel good about who they are—don't **own** who they are—for one reason or another. Those deeply rooted emotions, often universal, may stem from challenging childhoods, teenage traumas, or other dramas that have played out in their lives.

Those old experiences literally wire our brains, and new experiences fall into those same themes, reappearing with new names or situations. These negative tapes—limiting beliefs—play on looping recorders in our heads. If we allow those stories and tapes to continue to play in our heads, the lingering effects can diminish our confidence, preventing us from embracing who we are and going after what we deserve in our lives. We deserve to go after our dreams, to create our next chapters.

The good news is it is possible to get rid of those negative tapes. Yes, it will take courage, and yes, maybe it will require professional help, but it is possible. We can learn to change how we feel about ourselves. We can develop more self-esteem, and we can grow in confidence.

What's interesting about the work I do as a coach is that no matter how successful someone is, no matter what industry, regardless of gender, sometimes we all lack confidence, and our insecurities rear their heads up when we least expect them.

One of my New York clients had just gotten a promotion and was moving into a new prestigious role at his company. He'd been working toward this goal for a couple of years and was excited and ready for this next step. He should have been on top of the world, and yet, he was coming to me because he was struggling with the confidence and presence he felt he needed to take into this next chapter.

Confidence is a state of mind.

He found himself in uncharted territory, getting extremely nervous when he had to make any kind of presentation before senior leaders. This had never really happened before, and it began to have a huge impact in almost every area of his life, professionally and personally. It went so far that he was concerned that some form of depression was sinking in, and he simply didn't know how to stop the downward spiral.

While he admitted that perhaps a lack of preparation on his part for those speaking opportunities contributed to his nerves, he also stretched himself out of his comfort zone and really looked at where the insecurities were coming from. What buttons were being pushed? He had to find the courage needed to go deeper. For some, professional counseling may need to come into play to answer some of those deeper questions.

Life has taught me that confidence is a state of mind. Confidence is something that is learned as a result of experiences and how we've learned to react in different situations.

There are conflicting theories as to whether we are born with confidence or not, but one thing is certain: Confidence plays an important role in our lives.

In the book *The Confidence Code,* written by journalists Katty Kay and Claire Shipman, their research suggests, "Confidence is something we can, to a significant extent, control (2014, 239)." It can be acquired.

If this is true, then we can all—each and every day—make the decision to build up our confidence and find ways to create more of it.

But here's the kicker: A "healthy" sense of self-confidence is not something that we achieve once and then just have for the rest of our lives. It's not as if there is some set of rules that we must follow to be and stay confident. It's not static.

Confidence has an ebb and flow to it. It can increase and decrease. I call it the "confidence barometer." It can and does go up and down. There are some days we feel more confident than others, and that's great. We all have things we do well, and others we do *not* do so well, and that's okay. But there are steps we can take to minimize the swings of confidence.

It starts by owning who you are, *where* you are. That is the foundation. Trusting your own value. That can be a challenging concept for some because we try so hard to be perfect! We feel the need to want to cross every *t* and dot every *i*. This can be especially tough for women. The irony is striving for such perfection leads to hesitation, even paralysis, and we get nothing done. We ultimately hold ourselves back.

Perhaps it's our collective conditioning from our culture. Many women feel they must have all the perceived necessary experiences before ever going after a next-level role. Men, on the other hand, seem to simply go for it, regardless of whether they have crossed all the *t*'s and dotted all the *i*'s.

According to Kay and Shipman, there is absolutely a "confidence gap" that separates the sexes when it comes to looking to advance one's career. Women applied for a promotion only when they met 100 percent of the qualifications. Men, on the other hand, applied when they felt they met just 50 percent of the qualifications necessary.

In addition, women often worry that without the so-called right experience on their résumé, they may make some catastrophic mistake that will surely destroy their career and, therefore, they don't have the confidence to go for it.

It takes courage to go for it. It takes courage to be willing to fall and possibly fail.

Failure is Not Fatal

We all have failures. It's inevitable, especially when you are doing something new. We all make mistakes. But life is not about making mistakes. It's about the courage to *be* confident (or find your confidence) even when those things happen, or in spite of them.

I certainly have made my share of mistakes, even at times when I wanted to be at my best (and to be "perfect").

Six reporters from around the country were all present at ABC's network studios in New York. We were all there to interview Charlie Gibson, host of *Good Morning America.* I was honored to have been selected to represent my station and very excited to meet him. I respected him greatly professionally, and I was also a fan.

The night before my interview, while speaking with a network sports anchor friend of mine, I shared with him my trepidation and the nerves I was feeling. He told me not to worry and gave me a few suggestions of how to begin the conversation with Gibson. None of them felt right to me, but I didn't have the confidence to say that his suggestions weren't my style, that they wouldn't feel authentic. HE was the national network reporter, not me. He must, therefore, know more than me.

I was selected to go first. I don't recall what I said to start my interview, but all I do remember is that it felt totally wrong! Here I was, the largest market reporter, with all eyes on me, and I felt like I bombed. My recollection is that even Gibson seemed perplexed by my opening question. It was a very awkward moment.

I did manage to move on, but my confidence fell through the floor at that point, and all I could do was try to maintain some composure and save face. I also don't think I ever told my friend how awful it felt. I was simply too embarrassed, and for some stupid reason, I feared if I told him his idea missed the mark, I would hurt his feelings. And yet, I was the one mortified on the inside. Oh, brother, talk about limiting beliefs!

I wished I'd listened to my instincts and trusted myself more when it came to not going with the suggested humorous approach I took with Gibson. If my friend had delivered that opening question, coming from him it probably would have been great, but it wasn't me, and I knew it. I didn't listen to my gut. I didn't listen to my own voice, or even use my voice after the fact to tell my friend. I wasn't owning *me*. I was looking for validation outside of myself, and how often do so many of us do that? A lot!

When we don't own who we are, we are not being as authentic as we could be. Often it is out of a fear that we will somehow fail if we are that authentic. We will be ridiculed or judged negatively for our authenticity, perhaps because it's happened before.

It is sometimes scary to be authentic, to own who we are on the inside, but if we don't, we also may miss out on an opportunity to live our happiest, healthiest, best life, to live out our values.

Another time I felt as if I totally bombed came when I was asked to speak to a nonprofit organization on the topic of "How to Find Your Voice." The organizers specifically asked me to share my career journey, but about halfway through my speech, I could feel the energy was just not flowing from me to them, nor from them back to me. My gut was telling me to change course. Yes, change course right then and there. It was telling me to forget about what I'd planned to share with them and go with what I was feeling in that moment.

Now, as a communications coach, normally I would never recommend this to anyone, but this was one time I wished I had trusted myself more in that moment. When I got their survey feedback on my session, nearly 60 percent thought it was good to great, but the remaining 40 percent found it not so great. Disappointing, to say the least, but I already knew the results. No, no one is perfect. I'm certainly not, but I didn't trust myself enough. I felt like I failed them, and I failed me.

In hindsight, yes, they wanted to know how I used my voice to maneuver through my career, from singing to TV to my communications company. But what I wish I had done more of was to share with them how I have used my voice to advocate for others and what my intention is in this book: to help others find their voice, to own who they are. I kept that survey as a reminder of the lesson learned that day. It's always about them, your audience, whomever that may be, and not about you.

I'm not perfect, and I sometimes need to remind myself of my own words. Being imperfect is more perfect because you are being your best authentic self.

Failure isn't the enemy, not learning the lessons is the enemy.

While those experiences felt like failures, in many respects, they were not. They were important lessons that taught me about myself: how to strengthen my resolve, grow in confidence, trust my instincts, and trust myself more. But if I had beaten myself up after any of them, or the countless other so-called *failures* in my life, I wouldn't be where I am today. My mother often said to my brothers and me that it's not what happens to you but what you do with it that makes the difference.

The Fear of Failure

Failure isn't the enemy, but perhaps the *fear* of failing is. That can be more demoralizing to one's confidence sometimes than the actual failure itself.

Why are we so afraid of failure? Sure, we don't like it. Who does? As I shared with you in Chapter One, if I had allowed fear to stand in my way, I would never have launched my business, and if fear was the only reason I could think of not to do it, that was simply not a good enough reason.

Many have commented on failure and fear of failure. NBA great Michael Jordan said, "I can accept failure, everyone fails at something, but I can't accept not trying." Yes, we all must try.

There are so many times in my life when I didn't know how to do something. I didn't know how to do the weather on TV. I didn't know how to be a reporter, nor how to do breaking news. I didn't know how to launch a business, let alone run it, but I have always held fast to the belief that just because I've never done something before doesn't mean I can't. I just have to try.

Will I be good at everything I try? Hell, no! But that's not the goal, to be good or great at it ALL. Each of us is born with our own unique strengths. I believe those are our gifts from God, and it's up to us to figure out what those are, use them to be in service, and give back to the world, to fulfill our purpose.

So, while we may "fail" at something—we may even bomb!—failure isn't the enemy. Not learning the lessons is the enemy. I'm still learning, and as long as I am alive, I hope that I will continue to grow, to learn, and to at least try.

The point is to try. You will learn, and in some cases, you will learn what NOT to do in the future because now you are truly owning who you are. There may even be a new-found acceptance that your path lies elsewhere. That is okay too. You are moving toward being your best authentic self, and when you do that, it's possible to make dreams come true.

The Courage to Continue

Winston Churchill once said, "Success is not final, failure is not fatal: it is the courage to continue that counts."

Yes, confidence includes picking yourself up when you've fallen, knowing what to do—or figuring it out—when mistakes come to light, and despite it all, continuing on. But confidence is also about having the courage to be totally honest with yourself about what your strengths are and what your areas of growth are.

This is another major difference between men and women. Each gender assesses their skills very differently. Studies show that men overestimate themselves in their abilities and performance, and women underestimate themselves in **both** categories.

Confidence has the opportunity to blossom when you are willing to be courageous enough to honestly reflect on your skillset, your truth, and your value, and when you are willing to stop comparing yourself to other people. Perhaps comparisons are just a natural part of life, the competitive world in which we live, but if we can cultivate the ability and courage to trust ourselves and our value, and honestly reflect what we have to offer, our confidence will grow. Be confident knowing and believing you can create exciting new chapters, even without the so-called right experience on your résumé.

I don't have an MBA, yet I am running a successful business. My confidence continues to grow as an entrepreneur with each chapter, each opportunity, each experience. No knowledge is ever wasted.

My confidence has also grown by leaps and bounds when clients tell me that I have helped them grow in their own confidence from our work together.

One of my female clients was up for a big promotion when she started to work with me. I'll never forget our first session meeting. Her confidence was in the basement! This was the second time she was up for the same promotion, having been passed over the year before. She wasn't even sure she wanted to go through the process all over again out of fear she wouldn't make it.

While we spent a lot of time working on her business case, crafting the story of her presentation she would have to give before a panel of superiors, a great deal of energy went into exercises and techniques to help her find, create, and build up her confidence.

We also did a lot of work on getting past her need for perfection. Given that she felt like a complete failure for not having gotten the promotion the first time, she was sure she had to be perfect or else she would fail again.

As our engagement came to its conclusion, she knew she was ready for that big presentation day, and yes, she did get that promotion. Our time together was life-altering for her in so many ways, not the least of which was helping her discover her own confidence. At the conclusion of our engagement, she summed it up with this comment: "Your support truly changed my life. Working with you during the past two years has been nothing short of transformational—both professionally and personally."

I often see the progress before my clients do, the growth from session to session, but when they see it? When they feel it? *That* is the best feeling in the world. It's like the icing on the cake. That is a confidence-boosting moment for me!

So, ask yourself: What is holding me back? And what am I going to do about it?

There are many concrete ways for us to begin to build up our confidence and to learn how to have more of it.

For example, many people in the workplace assume that because they are competent enough in some arena they do not have to prepare for a meeting, a presentation, a virtual webcast, or even a conference call. That can potentially be a big mistake. If things don't go well, for whatever reason, that misstep can erode one's confidence. Everyone must prepare for the known and prepare for the unknown. Eighty percent of your success comes from preparation.

When working with my clients who know there will be live Q&A during a presentation or immediately following, we do a lot of role-playing. We discuss and consider what logical questions might be asked, but we take it a step further and consider what the "out of the box" question might be and have an answer ready. And if they don't know the answer, have a planned, prepared possible response. This is always fun for me because I get to use my TV interviewing skills in yet another new way. No knowledge is ever wasted.

Of course, you're never going to be able to predetermine every possible question that might come up, but I guarantee, if you practice anticipating out of the box questions, you will be that much more confident, even if you aren't able to answer them.

That's just one step. There are many ways that each of us, every day, can build up our confidence, especially on the days when that barometer has taken a bit of a dip.

- Start a task or project that you've been putting off for a long time. Or, in a to-do list, do the hardest task first, instead of the easy one. You will feel a sense of accomplishment. I can't tell you how many clients I work with who say to me that they always do the easy tasks first. By the time they get done with those, they are left with no energy and/or time to do the tough stuff.

- Be brave enough to ask a question at a public meeting, event, or in a group, but plan ahead. What could you ask that is relevant? What are you curious about?

- Even if you are petrified to speak up, volunteer to give a presentation or deliver a speech. If that is too much of an initial stretch, become a volunteer reader at your local library for children's story hour, offer to do a reading at your church, take voice lessons, or sign up for an improv class. All of these may feel like challenges, but they are opportunities to grow. With each "test" you are willing to take, you will get better. Your confidence will begin to expand.

- It could also be as simple as joining a group in your community or introducing yourself to someone new: at work, on the train, at your local coffee shop. Introduce yourself to the barista you see every morning. The point is, just start. Put yourself out there.

- Do not neglect the power of positive thought as a way to improve your confidence. The mind is a very powerful thing. As you have no doubt noticed in each chapter, I'm a big proponent of quotes and phrases to help me build up and maintain my confidence on those days that I may be feeling a bit low.

- Here is a personal game I came up with and have played with myself and shared with clients. I call it "My ABCs." I start at the beginning of the alphabet and think of a word for each letter that resonates with some form of confidence and how I want to *feel* about myself. For example: **A-** I am Authentic, I am Athletic, I am Articulate, I am Awesome! **B-** I am Bold, I am Brave, I am Beautiful. **C-** I am Confident, I am Creative, I am Connected to the Divine. And so on. I even try to see how many different adjectives I can come up with for each letter. This may seem like a silly game, but what you are doing is changing your energy, changing your thinking about yourself, and, little by little, creating new tapes in your head that are positive. You are affirming and owning who you are.

Every single one of these suggestions forces you to step out of your comfort zone. Think of it this way: We are all like rubber bands and are only willing to stretch ourselves so far because that is where we are comfortable. That is what we are used to doing. We get set in our ways, and the older we get, well, sometimes it makes it even harder to stretch that invisible rubber band. Don't get stuck! Stretch yourself!

And don't let the fear of failure stop you from taking on something new. If I had allowed the fear of failure to stand in my way, or the swings of my confidence barometer to dictate my actions, I would never have gotten into television, never have started my own business, never gone skydiving. I would never have written this book.

I have learned how to be confident. If I can learn how to be more confident and get out of my comfort zone, so can you. Find your courage to be confident!

Time To Reflect:

Boosting your confidence:

Besides doing all the exercises I just suggested, incorporate these as well.

Think back through your life and make a list of at least five times when you felt your least confident and a list of ten times—or better yet, more than ten—when you felt more confident. What connections can you make between those experiences?

Make another list of at least three things you are going to do to work on building your own confidence. And finally, what one thing will you do for yourself on the days when the confidence barometer takes a dip? Create your “go-to” trick or tricks to get yourself back on track. Maybe it’s a motivating quote, or reading a daily devotional, or having an inspirational app to look at, but always know what your “go-to” tricks are.

Facing Failure:

I encourage you to pick one or two moments in your life when you may have felt like a failure. Maybe you lost your job, or your presentation before your boss went off the rails and you choked, or an important relationship ended. You may even still feel the sting of that experience, and that’s okay.

No matter what happened, step back from yourself, put yourself in the “witness space,” and be very honest. What did you learn? What are you learning? How will you use that knowledge going forward in your life? Were you repeating old patterns of behavior, negative habits, because that’s all you know or knew at the time? Did you give 100 percent effort (your best shot), or could you have done more? Own the mistakes, if they are there, but be gentle with yourself.

You may not know the answers to all those questions at this moment but take the time to reflect. Write them down in your journal and come back to them if you need to. Allow the information and revelations to come to you.

When you stop trying to prove yourself to others or stop looking for validation outside of yourself and learn to trust yourself more, you are one step closer to owning who you are and living your best life.

5

Finding Your Voice

Find your voice and inspire others to find theirs.
~ Stephen Covey

My Authentic Voice

My heart was pounding so hard, it felt like it was going to jump out of my chest! It was 3:30 PM on Wednesday afternoon. Our news director was about to explain why he'd called the entire staff together for an important announcement.

Journalists are by nature a curious bunch! When the email went out asking the team to be present the next day for the meeting, of course, everyone was speculating. Although I'd been working behind the scenes with management on when my departure from WCVB would take place and how it would be announced, it was not public knowledge. What could it possibly be? My answer when asked? "It could be anything." I didn't want to lie.

As we all gathered, I wondered to myself, *Does anyone notice that I am the* ***only*** *anxious person in the room? Who knew that it would be hardest to share my news with THIS group of people?*

Our news director launched into his remarks, saying it's a sad day at NewsCenter 5 for they are about to lose someone who had been on every show at Channel 5 over the course of the past twenty years.

As he announced my name, I stood up from my chair, almost oblivious to the applause, and then I had this ah-ha moment. It suddenly occurred to me, *This is how most people feel when they get up in front of a group of people and need to speak!*

My heart was beating so fast, I thought I couldn't breathe... I felt the beads of perspiration on my forehead and hoped they didn't show... And in a nanosecond, questions filled my head. *Will I say the right thing? Will the words even come out of my mouth? Will I stumble? Will I feel or look like a fool? Am I making the biggest mistake of my life?*

The truth was by making it public knowledge I was about to leave, reality was setting in, and I was petrified! No turning back now.

I had to find my voice.

In that very instant, I realized I needed to rely on *everything* I'd learned in my nearly three decades of being on TV and in the public eye, which was exactly what I would be teaching my clients how to deal with at Brunner Communications. I knew I could and wanted to help others find their voice. Not only their "speaking voice," but their own authentic, inner voice.

I grew up in what I would describe as a very traditional, somewhat old-fashioned model of family where the man, the father, was the head of the household, no questions asked. As strong a woman as my mother was, given her own similar upbringing, Dad was the voice in our home. I often felt as if I couldn't express my authentic, inner voice.

Over the years, that resulted in my dad and me being like oil and water. We were often at odds over anything and everything. I remember one day being so angry about something—I have no recall of what today—but I remember the overwhelming, powerful feeling. I was on the floor of my bedroom, sobbing my eyes out because whatever it was that I wanted to say I felt I was absolutely not allowed to do so. I didn't have a voice or know how to use it. I couldn't speak my truth.

I'd be screaming on the inside when I wanted to be screaming on the outside.

The only way I was able to express myself was with tears, which were often misunderstood. I simply didn't know how to speak my truth, or I was too afraid to do so. I'd be screaming on the inside when I wanted to be screaming on the outside.

I didn't own my own voice, nor did I feel I was allowed to ever express or use my voice. (To this day, thankfully, I am not a screamer, never really have been and rarely, if ever, do I raise my voice in anger. Probably could have, or should have from time to time, but I guess that is one silver lining to come out of that experience.)

In many respects, I carried that limiting belief unknowingly into every area of my life, personally and professionally. It resulted, at times, in not knowing how to stand up for myself. All because I felt paralyzed on some unconscious level. There was a disconnect between my inner authentic voice and my outer voice. I feel like it's taken me years, and many therapy sessions, to break this pattern.

One of the first times I found the courage to speak my truth with my father was when I stood up for myself and went to Lawrence University, despite his initial opposition. It's so powerful when our inner authentic voice and our outer voice are in sync.

You've seen the words *limiting beliefs* in previous chapters. Let me add some clarity. Limiting beliefs are thoughts and feelings we carry with us from our life experiences. Some of them may develop during our childhood or possibly from a traumatic experience. They are often assumptions we make about ourselves that we come to believe as **fact**, but they may have absolutely zero truth to them.

If limiting beliefs get stuck in our psyche, they can impact our lives in negative ways. They can stop us from achieving more of what we are capable of, whether personally or professionally. Remember when I said in Chapter One that I didn't think I was smart enough to ever run a business? That is a limiting belief. (Why I didn't think I was smart enough, I really don't know.)

Liz Huber, a mindset and productivity coach, says, "We learn our belief systems as very little children, and then we move through life creating experiences to match our beliefs" (2018).

I've seen that theory play out numerous times as a communications coach. One of my Houston clients was really struggling with delivering presentations. He felt they were boring and monotone. He wanted to be more dynamic, engaging, commanding, and confident. In truth, what he was really asking for was how could he find his own authentic voice.

During our first session, I discovered several things that were hindering him from all of that and more. For one, he did virtually no preparation for any of his presentations. He chose to wing them every single time. In some cases, he didn't even know what the slides looked like that had been created for him to use until he first saw them up on the screen.

Perhaps more importantly was this: Here he was, a CPA, and yet he admitted to not enjoying being an accountant! Growing up, his dream was to build houses. But that was not an acceptable profession by his family's standards. He never allowed himself to express that desire. He became disconnected from his own authentic voice. And now, in a profession he really didn't want to be in, that limiting belief, that disconnect, was manifesting in not being a good public speaker. I think this was a form of unconscious self-sabotage because he really didn't want to be an accountant! And what better way to not be a successful presenter, public speaker, than by matching his inner belief with his outer experience.

I knew we had to find a way to minimize, or get rid of entirely, this unconscious belief that somehow he wasn't good enough, that he wasn't a good speaker. In truth, he wasn't as bad as he thought he was and wasn't giving himself enough credit for what he was doing well. Remember what I said in Chapter Two about often judging ourselves by what we think we are not?

Was there work to do to get him to another level when it came to his presentations? Absolutely, yes! Starting with being prepared and putting his message, his story, together in an interesting, compelling way, and practicing. He needed to incorporate Liz's 4 Cs:

- Be confident.
- Know your content.
- Have clarity of your content. In other words, can everyone understand your message?
- Deliver it in a conversational way.

By the end of our engagement, he had made major strides. He even admitted that maybe being an accountant wasn't so bad after all.

Perhaps you too may have an old belief that hinders you from believing that you have a voice worth finding, owning, and being heard. Perhaps you're afraid to use your own voice because you want to fit in or to please others—or even worse, you fear being rejected. It takes heart. It takes courage to find one's voice and own it.

This was probably why I began stream-of-consciousness journaling. I could safely write out my thoughts and feelings since I couldn't speak them out loud. I encourage everyone to journal. It can be a very cathartic, healing experience to go back from time to time and re-read your entries. Oftentimes, beautiful nuggets of truth come forth. There are often diamonds buried within your writings, lessons that you can take forward, if you are willing and brave enough to allow your authentic self to come through.

Your Voice as an Instrument

I once heard it said that the voice is the one instrument we all play. Unless you have a medical issue that prevents you from using your voice box or vocal cords, everyone has a voice.

It's unlike any other instrument. Your voice is internal. It's in your body. It's not something you can pick up and carry around, like a trumpet or violin. It's not an instrument that you sit down to play, like a piano or the drums. It's with you 24/7. Therefore, whatever is happening to you physically, emotionally, or mentally can and often does affect your voice. Nerves can wreak havoc on the voice, causing it to shake, quiver, or even disappear entirely, often happening at the worst possible times: trying to impress a boss, delivering a presentation, pitching a new client, or simply speaking in any public setting.

The voice is the one instrument we all play.

Think about it. None of us is born knowing how to get up and speak effectively in front of a group of people. It is a learned skill, one that can be improved upon by everyone.

No, you may not become a great orator. You may not sound like James Earl Jones or Dame Judi Dench, but you can get better, and you can learn skills and techniques to control the nerves, to make you more interesting, engaging, while still being your authentic self. (This is where a great coach can be a real asset! Or my online flagship course How to Be a Rock Star Public Speaker on BrunnerAcademy.com.)

For much of my life, I used my voice as a musical instrument. There have been times when I was lovingly teased about being a walking musical, bursting into song at any moment. I turned everything into a song.

My mother and father were both very musical, and that meant that my three younger brothers and I would, of course, be musical. From the time I was knee-high, there I was, singing in front of my father's congregation in the church choir and in every school vocal ensemble I could join.

All those voice lessons paid off too when I entered the Miss Marigold Pageant in Pekin, Illinois, a preliminary pageant to the Miss America Pageant system. I sang an operatic aria in each of the competitions—Miss Heart of Illinois and Miss Illinois—which ultimately led to my being in the Miss America Pageant. Although I didn't win that crown, I did earn enough scholarship money to pay for all my college education at Lawrence University Conservatory of Music. I was also one of the few vocalists chosen to perform at my commencement ceremony.

Music and singing filled almost every part of my life, from being in an opera company while in my teens, to teaching high schoolers how to sing, to touring and performing in Europe with The Park Forest Singers, a semi-professional chorale ensemble near Chicago.

We gave concerts in amazing cathedrals in Austria, Germany, Switzerland, Greece, and Italy. And we had the unique opportunity to sing for Pope John Paul II in Vatican Square. The sound system allowed our collective voices to fill St. Peter's Square. Even remembering that moment today gives me chills. It was exhilarating. I may be a Protestant, but I must admit, singing for the Catholic Pope was an experience I will never forget. I was but a few feet away from him as he came over to say hello and bless all of us.

There have been many memorable singing moments: performing our country's national anthem for several Boston universities and colleges and three of Boston's national sports teams (the Boston Celtics, the New England Patriots, and the Boston Red Sox).

For anyone who has ever attempted to sing "The Star-Spangled Banner," our national anthem, a cappella—which means with no accompaniment—it is not an easy song to sing, even if you are a trained singer. First, the range of notes stretches over an octave and a half. That is an extensive range. If you start too low or too high, you're in trouble! (For you musicians out there, my perfect key is A-flat.)

Secondly, if you are singing it a cappella, you better hope you start in the right key. I will use my pitch pipe for my starting note and pray that I stay on key and have no pitch issues… nerves will get you on that.

Even if you start in the right key, and have no pitch problems, then there are also the words to remember! Again, nerves can play a big part in remembering the lyrics. There have been many professional singers and celebrities who've messed them up, regardless of their experience and their practice!

But one of the hardest reasons of all to sing this song, especially if you are in an outdoor stadium—as I have been—is that there is often at least about a one to two second delay, if not more, which means there is a lag from what is coming out of your mouth to what is coming out of the speakers and back to your ears. It could be an entire line of the song. It's maddening because your inclination is to listen to yourself, which you can't—or shouldn't—do, because if you do, then you start to slow down, dragging the song down, and you never catch up! I've tried earplugs without much success.

People often ask if I get nervous. Absolutely, yes, I have! Wouldn't you under those circumstances? To sing before tens of thousands of people is daunting. *Just breathe, Liz... just keep breathing.* That's how I have tried to get through these performances. You might remember from Chapter One that I needed to do the same thing when I went skydiving for the first time.

A word of advice: If you ever get invited to sing the national anthem, practice, and do a sound check as well, especially if it's an outdoor stadium.

I've also had the honor and privilege of being on stage with the Boston Pops, under the direction of conductor Keith Lockhart. The Pops invited several radio and TV people, all trained singers, to perform in a benefit concert for a huge local charity event in Boston's Convention Center.

Our first and only rehearsal was in Symphony Hall. Wow! That was quite the experience. Its acoustics were amazing, and it was considered one of the three top concert halls in the world. Would I have ever guessed that I would someday sing in Symphony Hall, let alone with this prestigious orchestra? Nope, and it was the thrill of a lifetime!

I chose to sing "I Could Have Danced All Night" from the musical *The King and I.* I kept telling myself—as I did when I got my interview with President Obama (more on my long road to the White House still ahead!)—to just try to embrace this moment, be IN the moment and enjoy it. Yes, I was nervous that night too, but I tried to breathe through the nerves.

Making the transition from singer to news anchor/reporter was not that big a leap, and in many respects, quite natural. Singing is a skill, a form of storytelling, only with musical notes attached to the words.

If you've ever watched any of the talent shows like *The Voice* or *American Idol*, you hear the judges and coaches instructing the contestants to "tell the story."

I was still telling a story. I was still using my voice, but just in a different way. I was taking that skill set into my next chapter. Everything I'd learned about how to sing with good technique and stage presence accompanied and sustained me through my time in television and on various stages; it continues to carry me in presenting, keynote speaking, and all the way to coaching others to find their voices, something I once struggled with. While sometimes

I feel like I'm still learning, I, too, had to learn to use my voice, to speak my truth, to allow my authentic self to come through.

Perhaps it's one of the reasons I truly feel called to help others find their own voice. I've been there. I *get* it.

What's interesting about when someone first begins to find their inner voice and start using it: it may feel foreign, like an entirely new language. It's almost as if they go from one end of the spectrum to the other—from "silence" to "blasting" out their feelings in an almost aggressive way, as opposed to an assertive way. Everything is black and white, with no gray. They either don't say anything or what they *do* say comes out so strongly that it's misinterpreted.

Learning to create the gray, to find the appropriate balance between the two "voices"—being authentic and vulnerable and being strong and powerful—is important. It can be a steep learning curve and sometimes requires professional counseling too. It also takes practice and experience. Learning to use this powerful instrument, this authentic voice, can be a journey of personal and professional growth and lead to even greater confidence.

Being Seen and Heard

Just because you have a voice and can speak, does not necessarily mean you are being heard; *find your voice*.

Not feeling like you have been seen and heard can be demoralizing. It can strip away your confidence. If this is you, go back to Chapter

Three and really hone in on all the ways you can grow in your confidence and practice them.

More women may seem to struggle with being seen and heard, but trust me, based on my experience working with many clients—and that includes a lot of top-level, C-suite executives—this is another gender-neutral issue. Both sexes sometimes struggle to be seen and heard in the way they intend.

Given our differences, it's not surprising that there are so many misunderstandings and different expectations. We experience life and work very differently, we think differently, we cope differently, we communicate and speak differently! And while each gender's struggle may differ, the goal is the same. We all want to feel valued. None of us wants to be ignored. We all want to feel like our contributions matter. We all want to be seen and heard for who we are. It is a fundamental desire.

Finding your voice—having a voice—does not necessarily mean you need to be the loudest one in the room. What you should strive for is being a person who has influence, a leader who is willing to speak up, even if it's scary. That often involves being willing to get out of your comfort zone, again, and owning your authentic self. And more often than not, getting out of your comfort zone can be uncomfortable.

One of my friends, Terri Wein, is the cofounder of Weil and Wein, a career coaching company. Prior to starting this firm, she was a senior trader at a large investment bank.

One day, she told the president's assistant she needed to talk to her boss and asked the assistant to put her on the same plane with him the next day so they could go together to the big corporate dinner she'd been invited to attend. It was only then that she learned that was not possible because the boss was going down early in the morning for the golf tournament, to which she had NOT been invited before the dinner.

She asked the AA, "Please put me on his plane. I'm going!" And promptly marched down to her boss's office and told him she was going to the golf tournament. When he asked her if she played golf, she answered, "No, I don't! I start tomorrow."

Her boss then told her it was a "male-only" golf course. Her response, "I'm coming anyway." The boss then arranged—with less than twelve-hours' notice—to change the entire golf outing to a different club that welcomed everyone. She bought a pair of shoes in the pro shop, sat in the cart during the tournament, and participated in the conversations. She was being seen *and* heard.

The next week, the CEO of the bank called her into his office to thank her for speaking up and told her going forward, the bank would not fund outings at clubs that discriminate.

Now, that takes chutzpah! Terri pushed her way through any discomfort she may have had, and maybe even her boss had to do the same, initially. But that is sometimes what is required, as scary as it may be.

There are so many reasons why it may be hard to get out of that comfort zone. Maybe you want to impress your boss and you're afraid your voice won't even be heard if you do speak up. You may also feel like you are the only one in the room with these insecurities. But you're not! You are not alone.

While coaching one of my London clients, she told me how excited she was that she was finally being invited to attend some of the strategy meetings with more senior executives. However, her role was to simply take notes, even though she had been the developer of many of the strategies and projects that were being proposed and presented by those more senior leaders.

Trust that you have a role to play...

She had a seat at the table but was not being seen nor heard in a way that would showcase her valid and important contributions. She was afraid to speak up, afraid to use her voice, and was unsure how to do so in that situation.

I reminded her that because she knows all the details better than anyone in that room, she should plan to be ready to speak and to find a way to add to the discussion in the most confident voice she could find.

Trust that you have a role to play, a contribution to make, and that you have been invited to the table for a reason.

What you say, how you say it, and how you *sound* saying it matters. This is one of the techniques I work on with clients because your voice matters greatly.

Everyone needs to be ready to speak up, to find and to use that confident voice, which requires time and preparation before the meeting even begins. Mastering the pre-meeting requires two things.

1) Get there early because often "the meeting before the meeting" is where some of the real work happens. It's during the small talk that you get to know someone by connecting, building a relationship, and establishing a trust so that when you do speak up you are known, seen, and heard.

2) You must strategize before going into any meeting with a way to not only contribute, but also to add value to the conversation/ discussion, taking it another step forward, and if offering a point of view, being able to back it up with the "why."

To be seen and heard, one must use active words and authoritative statements. Be sure to fully explain why you agree, why you disagree, and why you are offering suggestions in your most accessible concrete language. The *why* is key.

- Replace "I think" or "I feel" with "I'm confident," "I'm convinced," or "I expect, and here's why…"
- Replace "How about x, y, or z?" with "I strongly suggest… and here's why…"
- Replace "I tend to agree" with "That's absolutely right and here's why…"
- Replace "Well, maybe we can…" with "Here's my plan…"
- Replace "Well, what if…" with "I recommend and here's why…"

One more important point: Stop apologizing or using minimizing language and negative qualifiers because they weaken your message.

In the listener's mind, you are not confident in the message you are sharing. Negative qualifiers can take away from your having an assertive, commanding, powerful voice, and message. The following language keeps you small; refrain from using words like "actually" or "just" or "I'm sorry" when you have nothing to apologize for. Another example is, "I'm no expert at this, but…"

When you can contribute and add value, you are seen as attentive, engaged, and as projecting presence and confidence; essentially, you are assisting in moving the conversation forward.

Now, you may need to practice your thoughts and ideas out loud, in private, before entering the room. Yes, practice! There's a muscle memory that takes place between the brain and the mouth when you practice out loud. No, do not memorize your comments, but know them well enough to be comfortable with the words so they flow out of your mouth confidently.

By the way, the same holds true for any remarks you may have to give, a pitch you must make, a presentation, or an acceptance speech for an award. Practice! Practice! Practice! And use Liz's 4 Cs: confidence, content, clarity of your content, and deliver it in a conversational way.

Liz's 4 Cs:
Confidence
Content
Clarity
Conversational

It's reported that Mark Twain said, "It takes three weeks of preparation in order to sound spontaneous." You may not literally have three weeks, but the point is, preparation and practice are key.

As a news anchor, I could always tell when a producer or writer had not read their script out loud. Sure, it may have been wonderfully written prose, but often it wasn't conversational or easy to read out loud, which is what an anchor needs to gain the trust of the viewers.

I didn't always have the luxury of time to read every script out loud, but I had *years* of practice and a skill set that allowed me to deliver those stories well, with vocal variety and with the right tone and inflection for the content, even if I hadn't practiced and had to read a script "cold."

I must admit, whenever I saw the words "attempted abduction" on the teleprompter, I knew to SLOW down. Those two words together were, for me, difficult to say swiftly. Try it yourself and you'll likely see what I mean; the combination of the consonants can be challenging.

What's been fascinating over the past few years is the explosion of audiobooks and podcasts. People are drawn to the emotion heard and felt in a human being's voice. A creative and expressive voice is such a powerful communication tool.

In author John Colapinto's book *This is the Voice,* he suggests that, "The soul, in some sense, resides in the larynx" (2021) What a beautiful way to think about our voice and soul almost being one.

When we get in touch with our soul, when we are still enough to hear that inner voice, we can begin to take steps to have it become our outer voice, our speaking voice.

But often there is so much noise going on all around us, or we consciously or unconsciously distract ourselves, that we can't hear that inner voice and, therefore, can't own that inner voice. We may even question whether that inner voice is truth or something else.

Steve Schlafman is a coach, angel investor, and self-described "recovering VC" (venture capitalist), and he offers up this powerful thought: "Listen to your inner voice, not your inner critic" (2018). Love that, but I also know that is sometimes not very easy to do.

Finding your true, authentic voice takes great practice and time. Be gentle with yourself; it doesn't happen overnight. When you can integrate what's on the inside—the truth from your heart, mind, and body—and express it on the outside, you will live a more authentic life.

So just start because when you do, you can make dreams come true and create an amazing next chapter.

Time To Reflect:

Journaling:

Journaling has been found to have a profound effect on relieving stress, boosting your immune system, clarifying thoughts, even resolving problems. Therefore, it's important that you don't censor yourself. I highly recommend it. Write down your innermost thoughts as they come to you, expressing anything—without judgment and without trying to sound a certain way. Your feelings are your feelings, they are not right or wrong. I recommend you try journaling, privately. The words you write are for your eyes only. In doing so, you will learn things about yourself that you may never have known otherwise.

You could start out by reflecting on some of your goals, hopes, dreams, and why they feel important to you. Pay attention to what makes you feel alive.

Questions you could ask of yourself might start with something like this: In what areas of my life am I being truthful? In what areas am I being less truthful? When speaking with family and friends, what truths might I be withholding and why? Which voice am I listening to, the inner voice or the inner critic? What ways am I finding to quiet the distractions so I can hear that inner voice?

Also, begin to pay attention to when you may unknowingly betray your own voice. For example, ask yourself: Am I walking my own path, or am I following what someone else expects of me? (We'll talk more about that in Chapter Eight.) Or do you find it hard to say no? If you are always saying yes because you are too afraid to say no out of fear of disappointing someone, that's a betrayal.

Explore your own relationship with *no* through journaling. Learn to say "No!" Take on only the commitments you have time for or that you truly care about. When a request is made, is it something you really must attend to, or can you delegate it to someone else? Learn not to feel guilty about saying no. Setting boundaries is never easy, but if you value your time, others will too.

I've been journaling for more than thirty-five years now, and I truly believe that my inner voice speaks to me if I am willing to listen. Others also report having the same experience; I encourage you to try it.

Just as there are no right or wrong feelings, there is no right or wrong way to journal. There is no right or wrong amount of time to devote to it. Some days, you may write more than others, and that's okay. Just do it. The more you make it a practice, the easier it will become and the more you will find your own inner authentic voice.

Meditation:

Too often people get hung up on trying to meditate "correctly." Don't! If you can be quiet with yourself for even ten minutes—sitting, breathing, and trying to be still—you are meditating.

Because there are so many different types of meditation, don't be afraid to keep trying different versions until you find one or two that do fit. I personally don't think it matters which one you choose, as long as it feels right for you.

Besides books on the subject and classes you can take in-person or virtually, there are also many apps available that can help you on this journey.

Yes, thoughts will and often do come into your mind, but as Tamara Levitt from the Calm app ALWAYS says, just come back to the breath.

The point is to try to create a sense of internal peace so that you can hear your thoughts and recognize—honor—your inner, most authentic voice. Good luck!

If you'd like to explore meditation a little bit further, I invite you to check out my Dare: To Find Peace of Mind course on BrunnerAcademy.com.

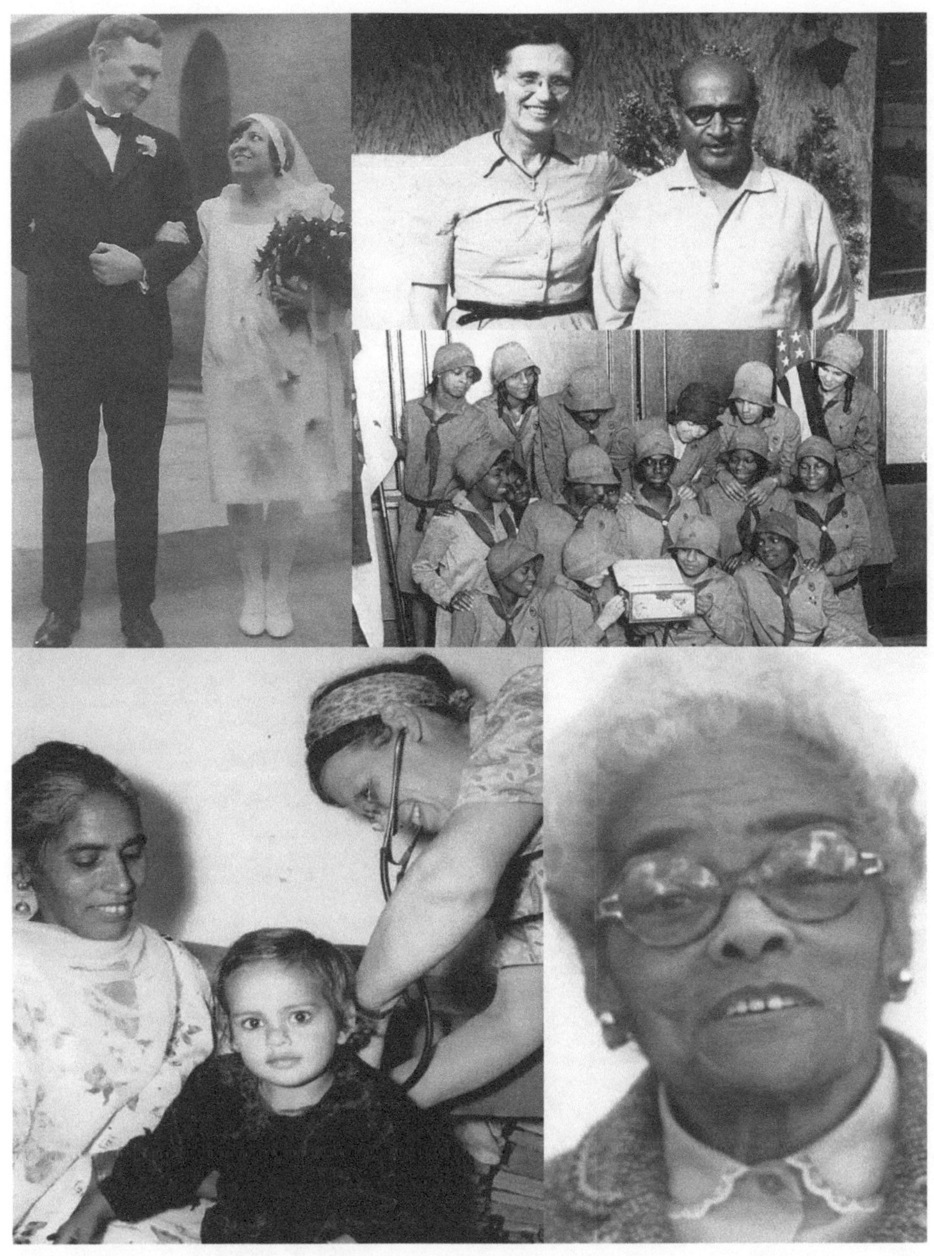

From top left (clockwise): Rev. & Mrs. Galen E. Russell, Sr., Paternal Grandparents; Doctors C. Joseph and Dorothy Dunning Chacko, Maternal Grandparents; Mrs. Galen Russell, Sr. (Grammie) with her Girl Scout Troop in Harlem; Godmother, Dr. Abbie Clement Jackson; Dr. Dorothy Chacko with young patient.

From top left (clockwise): Miss Illinois, 1979; Performing with the Boston Pops, 2015; With mom, Mary Chacko Russell, 2010; National Anthem, Boston Red Sox, 2014; National Anthem, Boston Celtics, 2014.

From top left (clockwise): Dancing with Tony Dovolani, 2011; With David Muir; Skydiving, 2015; On the WCVB anchor desk, Courtesy WCVB; Reporting with David Muir, WCVB, 2003; Guest appearance as a waitress on soap-opera *All My Children*.

From top left (clockwise): Marshall Goldsmith, 2019; Oprah Winfrey, approximately 1985; Vatican Square with Pope John Paul II, 1983; Tom Brady, NFL Quarterback, 2015.

From top left (clockwise): At the White House, 2013; "Bo," the Obamas' dog, 2013; Interviewing President Obama at the White House, 2013.

From top left (clockwise): Barron's Women Summit, 2018; *Boston Common Magazine*, "In Liz We Trust," 2013; Daring to Own Brunner Communications; The most common pre-broadcast look – curlers.

Own Your Dreams

SECTION TWO

6

Be the Leader Within

Before you are a leader, success is all about growing yourself. When you become a leader, success is all about growing others.

~ **Jack Welch**

Defining Leadership

Have you ever heard the phrase, "He (or she) is a born leader"? I don't believe that to be entirely true. Just as we are not born knowing *how* to speak effectively in front of a group of people, we are not born knowing *how* to be a leader. We *learn* how to lead from our culture, environment, experiences, parents, teachers, and even books.

While coaching clients, I've witnessed firsthand the urgency that exists in developing new leaders and empowering them so that companies stay relevant, retain great talent, and continue to be successful in the future. Good leadership is an essential key to corporate success; however, the leadership and management needs of companies have changed. Leadership now needs to occur at all levels of a company, not just at the top.

My philosophy is that we all have the qualities within us to lead, but for whatever reason we may not reach our full potential, either by choice or because we may get trapped focusing on the wrong things. It was Henry Ford who said, "You don't have to hold a position in order to be a leader." That's what happens though; too many people get caught up in titles or organizational charts.

True leadership has nothing to do with a title, nor does having the responsibilities of a leader necessarily make someone an *effective* leader.

Leadership is about relationships. Effective leaders are skilled practitioners of relationships. They know how to get people to do things they wouldn't ordinarily do. They inspire a can-do attitude of "How do we get it done?" and "Let's go and do it." They are able to deliberately create and challenge results by enlisting the help of others. By developing more leaders within the organization, they have the power to change a company's culture.

Leaders help others perform at their best. According to John Quincy Adams, "If your actions inspire others to dream more, learn more, do more and become more, you are a leader."

How do they do it? What's their secret?

Perhaps, more importantly, you may be asking yourself: How do I become that kind of leader? How do I become my own leader within?

Successful leaders do tend to have certain traits. During workshops, I often ask participants what are those traits and characteristics of a good leader? How do they define leadership?

Harry Kramer is an executive partner with Madison Dearborn Partners, a private equity firm based in Chicago, Illinois, and a Clinical Professor of Strategy at Northwestern University's Kellogg School of Management. I had the opportunity to hear him present the themes of his book *Becoming the Best: Build a World-Class Organization Through Values-Based Leadership* (2015). In it, he outlines his four principles to becoming a value-based leader: self-reflection, balance, true confidence, and genuine humility. He believes if you make progress in these four areas, you will become a better leader.

While Kramer's four principles are important, my colleague Candy O'Terry and I believe there are six additional very important traits that one must have and harness to become a powerful leader: competence, trustworthiness, the ability to motivate and inspire, passion, authenticity, and vision. Candy chose the image of a star to illustrate the six leadership points we call "Leadership Presence is Star Power."

Imagine a star with its five points. Each point on that star represents a successful leadership trait. At the center of the star is competence, the core of our Leadership Presence is Star Power symbol. It is the ability to do the job well. You have the skill set needed. However, being competent doesn't necessarily mean you know *how* to do everything, but rather, you have the ability to know *what* to do and *how* to get it done.

Competence and trustworthiness are inextricably linked because it really doesn't matter how competent you are; without trust, you won't get very far as a leader.

Trustworthiness is the first point of the star. Being trustworthy and being *seen* as trustworthy means your words and your actions are in sync. When your teams trust you, you have a better chance of reaching your goals. Your teams become committed and motivated.

Star point number two: A true leader is able to motivate and inspire. They move people to act in a way that achieves a specific goal. Why do you think coaches give pep talks to their teams? They become motivated to win.

Just as in sports, motivation plays a key role in employee productivity. An effective leader understands the different factors and needs of subordinates to motivate and inspire them. He/she must be what I call "a good student of human nature" which is what made me a good journalist. (It's also one of the reasons I have been successful as a coach.) When you only have three minutes for an interview, you must understand human nature very well. You must have a sharp perception of *how* to connect with someone very quickly. Having sharp perception allows you to read people's signals and react appropriately. In other words, effective leaders must *know* their employees.

Passion is the third point on the star. Effective leaders bring a sense of passion to everything they do and ignite it in others, and that energy is contagious. People want to follow a passionate leader. It's not only passion for a project, the company, or its people, it's a passion for life. Authors Robert Kriegel and Louis Patler cite a study of 1,500 people over twenty years that highlights five things that happen when a leader is passionate: passion produces energy, drives vision, ignites others, raises influence, and provides potential (2012).

Authenticity is the next star point. Authentic leaders are not afraid to tell their story and to reveal who they are to others. There is never a question of what they stand for. When leaders are willing to share their experiences and, just as importantly, *listen* to others' experiences, a connection is made. Not only are authentic leaders not afraid to express themselves honestly, but they are also not afraid to ask the difficult questions and act accordingly. As the *Harvard Business Review* declared in January 2015, "Authenticity has emerged as the gold standard for leadership." I believe that is even more relevant today.

And finally, great leaders bring vision, the fifth point. They can see the goal, the finish line, with a clear understanding of what it takes to get there. This is the essence of leadership. They not only share their dream and the direction in which to go, but they also inspire people to want to follow that vision.

Jack Welch certainly knew how to do that. As former chairman and CEO of General Electric between 1981-2001, he was famous for saying, "Good business leaders create a vision, articulate the vision, passionately own the vision, and relentlessly drive it to completion"

(2020). That philosophy bolstered the company's value by 4,000 percent during his tenure.

And no matter what your leadership skills and abilities are today, you can always learn to be a better, more effective leader. Becoming a leader is about becoming a full human being.

It starts by being more self-aware—self-aware of what your strengths are and an honest assessment of where your weaknesses lie and the areas in which you need to grow. I refer to them as "development opportunities." Ask yourself: What are my capabilities? What are my limitations? What are my goals? What makes me different and unique from my peers?

I ask workshop participants to rate themselves as to where they stand on many topics related to leadership. Is it a strength or a development area? For example, can you say, "I'm sorry," "I don't know," or "I was wrong"? Can you emotionally handle that not everyone will be supportive of the fact that you are the leader or *how* you are leading? There may be subtle or sometimes overt hostility toward your leadership style. It is not a question of "if" but most likely "when" that may happen.

Becoming a leader is about becoming a full human being.

Yes, people are more inclined to do business with you, to follow you, if they like you, but being an effective leader is not about if people like you. It's about focusing on the right things, at the right time, in the right way, for the right reasons, and with the right people. Being a leader is about having self-direction, knowing how to get things done, being organized, and avoiding procrastination. At times it requires making decisions quickly and at the same time considering all options on the table.

That became very apparent when the world was hit with the pandemic: COVID-19. We quickly learned who were the true leaders and who only held that title.

COVID-19 has been a critical stress test. It challenged every contingency plan and risk mitigation strategy every leader has ever had in place. In times of crisis, the way we manage teams and inspire those around us has a tangible effect on our ability to face a challenging and volatile environment. In the early days of the pandemic, when the world was brought to a standstill, businesses sent workers home. No one knew how long this was going to last. Everyone was moving through a fog of uncertainty.

How does one lead when you can't see the road ahead? Or when you don't know where the road ends? We had no known "liberation day," and it became very clear with each passing month this was going to be a marathon, not a sprint.

The lockdown phase was just the acute part of the crisis. The aftermath may bring longer turmoil. Only time will tell when we are back to normal, if ever.

Leaders needed to adapt, and in some cases, they needed to completely change their approach.

Annette Comer is a global leadership mentor, author of *Rescue Me! How to Save Yourself (and Your Sanity) When Things Go Wrong,* a top-level executive who spent twenty years in the corporate world, and now, in her next chapter, a coach of other leaders.

I interviewed her in June of 2020 for my podcast *Live Your Best Life with Liz Brunner*. She was quick to point out that the world had been brought to its knees as a global entity and the ways of doing business were changing dramatically. Everyone was being forced to face the questions of what is working and what is not working. At the same time, it provided us with an opportunity to focus on what makes a leader and a business successful.

In almost every leadership workshop I do, I share this quote from author George Fraser, who is considered to be an iconic voice of leadership and one of the world's top authorities on networking and effective relationships: "Business is about relationships. Without relationships you have no business. Without relationships you have no business being in business. In fact the business you're really in is the business of building relationships" (Conner 2014).

Networking is one of the most important skills you can learn to master when it comes to your professional and personal success.

When I launched my business, I knew I needed to practically rebrand myself. This was my next chapter, and I needed people to see me in a new light and hear from me about what I was doing to help people, not only with their overall communications skills but to find their authentic voice.

A few weeks into this new chapter, I opened *The Boston Globe* and saw a huge full-page ad for the *Boston Business Journal's* Power 50 event, an annual networking event honoring that year's selected most powerful fifty people in Boston. As I surveyed the list of honorees, I realized I knew more than half the people on that list. I promptly bought a ticket and went, alone.

It was a great opportunity for me to reconnect with people I had met over the years, whether through a story or a charity event. It was all about connecting and being willing to step out of my comfort zone and meet new people too. As it turned out, unexpectedly, one of my first big corporate clients came out of my attending that one event.

I pushed myself through what is often an uncomfortable situation. I really had to be brave and confident.

Many people are often uncomfortable with traditional networking events. All that small talk can sometimes feel like dating because there may be so many awkward conversations. And when the world was in lockdown because of the pandemic, people didn't seem to know what to do to network, let alone how.

There are three types of networking.

1) Operational Networking: This is about building and maintaining relationships with people you do business with on a regular basis.

2) Personal Networking: These are people who support your personal development. They are usually outside of your

current company. They can also help you find the support you need during professional or personal rough patches.

3) Strategic Networking: This is building a relationship to enhance and achieve your professional goals and your sphere of influence (Golden n.d.).

No matter which type of networking, whether in-person or virtual, participating in networking is one thing, and making the most of it is another. I've developed a three-step approach that works. It begins with the pre-game—doing your homework before the event. For example, homework may include finding out who else is attending the same event, which may include asking for a guest list from the host. Then comes game time—what you do once you are in the room, how to do "small talk" well, how to connect with people and be a resource for them. And finally, post-game—what you do to follow up because if you are not following up, you are not networking.

Networking is **not** about making the sale, but rather how can you be of value in someone else's life.

I lead entire seminars on networking, which are a lot of fun because they are very interactive; people get to practice their newly learned skills right then and there, whether during the seminar or in an after-seminar cocktail party.

So, when you participate in your next networking event, how will you approach it? Will it be time well spent or a missed opportunity? You get to decide.

IQ vs. EQ

Forming, maintaining, and sustaining relationships and being a true leader is more often about the soft skills than the hard skills. We're talking about your EQ (emotional quotient) or as it's sometimes called your EI (emotional intelligence).

Howard Gardner, the influential Harvard theorist, has written a lot about EQ and suggests how well you do in your life and career is determined by both your IQ *and* EQ. Simply having a high IQ is not enough for success. Being "book smart" is not the same as being "people smart."

And psychologists generally agree. According to research, among the ingredients for success, IQ accounts for roughly **10-20** percent (at best 25 percent); the rest depends on everything else—including EQ (2017).

Leaders with a high EQ are intrinsically more self-aware. They listen and communicate clearly, encourage creativity, and offer new challenges with ample support to achieve goals. They manage performance effectively by setting expectations clearly and concisely, and they also have empathy. Some companies such as Cisco Systems, Inc., Ford Motor Co., Tesla, and LinkedIn have gone so far as to invest in empathy training to improve management, retain employees, or guide design decisions.

My experience with some top-level leaders has shown me that both empathy training and EQ coaching is crucial. Have you ever heard the phrase, “This one is a tough nut to crack”? That was my first impression of one of my new clients. I’d been assigned by his company’s leadership program to be his coach for eighteen months, and I knew I had my work cut out for me the moment I met him. (Talk about forming first impressions of someone in the first three to five seconds!) I was up to the challenge, but I honestly didn’t know whether I would ever make any headway with him.

This man may be one of the smartest people I have ever met. For all I know, he truly is a genius and a member of Mensa, the high IQ society… and he never let me forget it. He had no patience for what he called “stupid, incompetent people,” by whom he believed he was surrounded every day. He was a very senior leader, a high level, successful performer within his company, destined for even greater opportunities ahead, which was why he was in this future leaders’ program. However, as high as his IQ probably was, what he was lacking was EQ, his emotional quotient or emotional intelligence.

It wasn’t long into our engagement that I knew I had to delicately bring up this topic, which I felt would not be the first time he’d been told he needed to work on his softer skills. It wasn’t! But again, just as he had no patience for people who he didn’t deem as smart as he was, he really didn’t care that anyone thought he needed to work on his bedside manner. In his mind, his EQ was not the problem, everyone else was.

It would be months and months of working together, of me finding new and different ways to open his eyes to the fact that this one piece alone could potentially stand in the way of how he was being perceived, and thus, negatively impact the trajectory of his career path. As a result, he would not reach the kind of success that he wanted and felt he deserved.

In my opinion, he needed to be willing to show more compassion, more emotion, and vulnerability. He needed to allow the authentic “human” leader within to come to the surface. He needed to be able to express some of the nuances that are often required in relationships with colleagues, subordinates, and even his superiors. It wasn’t that he couldn’t do it. He simply didn’t want to, nor did he feel he needed to.

I was so concerned about whether any progress was taking place that I had a conversation with one of the program’s organizers about what I was encountering. Careful to respect my client’s confidentiality and trust, I didn’t share everything, but enough to help the organizer understand what I was up against. He was not surprised. In hindsight, I think I was assigned to this coachee because the organizers may have felt if anyone could get through to him, maybe I could. I guess it was a compliment, but at the time, I was simply hoping I would be able to help this man. I knew I had to meet him where he was in order to help him grow.

I truly wanted him to be more successful, to be the “leader within” that I believed was there, but that would mean he would have to make some behavioral changes. And I honestly didn’t know if he would. It wasn’t until nearly the end of our assigned engagement that I had a hint that he respected me, trusted me, and seemed willing to implement some of the things we had worked on together. He asked if we could stay in touch and if I would be willing to continue to coach him going forward. Truly, I didn't see that one coming!

Not only did we continue to do quarterly check-ins for the next year, but he also sent several women to my Executive Coaching Workshop for Women and had several members of his team register for my flagship public speaking course on my online learning site, BrunnerAcademy.com.

My goal was to continually trust myself and my own instincts about how to connect with him and hopefully, eventually move the dial—and to find a way into and under that "superior persona" he sometimes hid behind.

I ended up becoming quite fond of this man, who I was initially sure thought of me as one of those "incompetent people" he was forced to work with! Who knew we would come full circle together! I learned from him, and I believe he learned from me too. That's what I call a win-win.

Themes and Patterns

If we demonstrate more of the principles of leadership, then no matter what role or position we hold, we can all be the leader within. But it requires true introspection and probing of what you believe in and why, and from where this belief comes. This is your leadership philosophy.

It begins by discovering the themes and patterns of your life. These themes—common threads—run through our lives like rivers or patterns that repeat themselves. They can be found in major life events, happy or sad memories, or even in your choices of movies, books, TV shows, artwork, Broadway plays, music… anything that has had an influence on you.

When you begin to recognize and acknowledge your unique themes and patterns, you will begin to discover *your story,* which creates a connection between the way you move through the world, the people you include in your inner circle, and even the career choices you have made. When you begin to connect all those dots, what's revealed is a leadership philosophy. It sets a direction for how you want to lead. It translates your values into action.

It gives me great pleasure to work with a client and guide them in not only discovering what their themes and patterns are, but how it leads to figuring out what their leadership philosophy is and how they arrived at that concept.

One of my San Francisco clients told me he was asked to speak at his alma mater about his career path. As he started to share his remarks with me, not surprisingly, as many people seem to want to do, he started in chronological order. I first did this, and then I moved on to that, and then I did this… blah, blah, blah! It sounded like a résumé laundry list!

A few minutes into his dialogue, I suggested we come at this from a different angle. I began by asking him a series of questions. When he was growing up, what did he want to be? What are his hobbies, etc.? After some discussion, I learned he was a baseball fanatic! He even found time in his off hours to be an umpire for Major League

Baseball. He loved statistics because 2 + 2 always = 4. The numbers don't lie. And he loved the rules of the game. He was a rules guy, so much so that he thought about becoming a police officer, but one night one of his fellow card-playing partners, who was a law enforcement officer, didn't show up for their weekly game. He later learned that officer was nearly killed in a gunfight. That was the end of that career path idea.

As I continued to work with him, we discussed each of his career steps from CPA to a comptroller, to auditor, to his current role as an inspector and expert witness in the financial industry. What emerged was a clear pattern of themes: numbers, rules, and a deep devotion to the idea that things be just and right. We completely reworked his speech and crafted an amazing story that was received by his audience with resounding success. They hung on every word.

For more than twenty-two years, one of my Florida clients had held many prestigious leadership roles in her firm, even spearheading projects with some of their global partners. When we began working together, she had just taken on a new role and felt she had landed smack in the middle of what some might call a "good ol' boys' network." It was important to her to not only be seen and heard but to contribute in ways that were meaningful and valuable.

It was not always easy. Even though she'd been at the company for nearly two decades, and had proven her expertise repeatedly, at times she felt as if some of those more senior leaders didn't take her seriously, in part because her background was not at all like theirs, nor those who had come up through the traditional ranks at the firm.

She was an English literature major, not an accountant. She felt like an outsider.

Over the course of our more than two-years engagement, her role changed many times, and with each new chapter came new responsibilities. It was challenging because just as she was settling in, her responsibilities and role would change. Again.

What helped her move from role to role, and chapter to chapter, was to step outside of herself and connect the dots of all her life experiences. She needed to uncover what her themes and patterns were, what skills existed hidden in those patterns, and to think about them differently.

Through our work together, she discovered that what made her different was what also made her valuable, and that sometimes being an "outsider" can be a good thing.

I recently heard from this client who happily shared with me that she had retired from the company and was about to embark on her next chapter in the private sector. She sent me this lovely message:

"I wanted you to know how much of an impact you made on me… so much of what we worked on together will be transferable to this next chapter—from articulating my unique brand proposition to finding my voice to telling a compelling story. Thank you, thank you, thank you for believing in me—your support has been amazing."

Thankfully, I have a pretty darn good track record, but have I been 100 percent successful with every client? No, no one is perfect.

Coaching is a two-way street, which means I need to meet the clients where they are, and they need to be open, and yes, vulnerable, and willing to make changes in their behavior and habits. That is a very tall order for some, and quite frankly, there are those who are simply not willing to change. (Remember what I said in Chapter Three: You must be ready on an emotional level to make any kind of change.)

Do I feel like I failed these clients? No, for two reasons: one, it's part of acceptance, and owning who I am. Disappointing, yes, because as much as I may have the best intentions and truly want to help everyone who comes to work with me, I may not be able to. And you know what? That's okay. One size does not fit all. And number two, what I learn from those clients are new ways to help other clients who are reluctant. In the teaching process, I am taught too.

Video cameras are a "truth tool."

One such initially reluctant client needed to present his business case for his promotion. He was absolutely convinced that he was a great presenter. Not because people had told him so, but because he believed he knew more than anyone else about how to share his story. While I'm all for having a healthy sense of self-confidence, there was a reason his company felt he needed my help.

During our first session together, I said, "Okay, let's hear it." As he began to deliver his content, I was so glad my videographer was with me, recording his presentation. I use video cameras in almost all my in-person coaching sessions because the camera never lies.

It is the "truth tool." (Just as there is instant replay in sports, I have my own instant replay.)

Being a good student of human nature, and a good coach, I was pretty sure I needed him to come to his **own** conclusion that his style of storytelling and mode of presenting was not the best, and not working at all.

As we began to review the video recording, I asked him what he noticed. What did he **like** about his delivery and performance? I intentionally ask people what they like because most people tend to pick out what they don't like or perceive to be their faults, things they did wrong. We hadn't gotten more than two minutes in when he said to me, "It's really boring." Truth tool. Yup, it was very boring. It sounded like yet another chronological dissertation instead of who this man was, what value he brings to the company, and how he can use his skills in other ways that he had not thought of. All of that—his value, using his expertise in new ways—was what was going to take him into this next chapter, his new role, and be successful at it.

I knew he had grown up in Europe, and I asked him to tell me about his childhood experiences. Little by little, themes and patterns began to emerge, all of which were so relevant to where he was at that point in his life, his abilities and skills, and yet, initially, he was extremely reluctant to change his presentation, his style of constructing and delivering his remarks.

It took some convincing, but once we began playing around with the content, getting more creative, implementing my storytelling concepts, and recording various new versions, he began to see and hear—thanks to the truth tool—how much better it was and how much more interesting it was. With each session, he began to come around and look forward to our work together.

His last session with me was but a few days before he would deliver his remarks. This time, we recorded the entire presentation from start to finish, something we hadn't done yet because we had worked on it in sections and backwards. (Yes, I have a methodology I've developed about how to practice backwards, and it works!) When we played the video for review, I could see his eyes light up! His face beaming with pride, he heard himself speaking with such passion, presence, and energy, owning his authentic self.

And, yes, he got the promotion and was told that it was a unanimous decision and that his presentation was one of the top presentations over the course of two days and fourteen candidates. His dream of his next chapter was now reality, and for me, another icing-on-the-cake moment.

In my own life, my themes and patterns didn't become quite so obvious until I began to connect my own dots. I'm a risk-taker—a calculated risk-taker, or as I like to say, an intelligent risk-taker. (Remember Chapter One: Jumping Off a Cliff!) I'm a teacher, coach, communicator, and motivator. Every career step I have taken has incorporated one or all these themes. No knowledge is ever wasted.

These themes and patterns of our lives craft and create our story. These stories don't simply explain what happened to us, but rather *why* they are important and *how* they shaped us. They give us a deeper understanding of who we are and how to be better leaders.

No matter where you are today, you can become a better leader. It is a choice.

And if your dream is to be seen as a leader, then I challenge you, as Harry Kramer challenges everyone, to ask yourself: Do I really want to be a leader? How proactive do I want or need to be to make being a leader a reality? Often, it requires getting out of one's comfort zone. Remember my rubber band theory in Chapter Four, The Courage of Confidence? As creatures of habit, we are only willing to stretch ourselves so far, but to grow and develop into being more of our authentic leader selves, we must stretch that rubber band far beyond what's comfortable.

If you are willing to stretch yourself, if you choose to lead and can lead yourself, you can lead other people. The leader within you will rise.

Time To Reflect:

Are you a leader?

Where do you stand when it comes to the six leadership qualities outlined in the star: competence, trustworthiness, motivation and inspiration, passion, authenticity, and vision?

What are your strengths? What are your development opportunities from your perspective?

And would your superiors, colleagues, or direct reports agree with your evaluation of yourself? Very often how we think we are being perceived may not be an accurate assessment.

Themes and Patterns:

Discovering the themes and patterns of your life often takes some time. This is also where a coach can be very helpful in guiding you on this journey. Begin by thinking back on your childhood.

- What did you want to be when you grew up? What were your hobbies? How did you spend your time?
- What were the pivotal moments in your life? Were those decisions made by you or someone else?
- Who were the most influential people in your life back then, and who are they now? Do you see any similarities between them?
- What have you learned about yourself in each job you have held?

Now, take all that information and see if you can begin to recognize any patterns, any themes. As you connect the dots, not only will they tell you about who you are, but also your own leadership philosophy will be revealed.

This is just the beginning of discovering your themes and patterns. Take the time to really be authentic and vulnerable and see what "leader" rises to the surface… whether professionally or personally.

7

Leadership Influence

Leadership is not about titles, positions, or flowcharts. It's about one life influencing another.

~ John C. Maxwell

Manager vs. Leader

When presenting my leadership workshops, one of the topics we discuss is the differences between being a manager and being a leader. Yes, a manager can have leadership qualities, but there are some subtle differences that come into play.

Management often consists of controlling a group or a set of entities to accomplish a goal. However, leadership refers to an individual's ability to influence, motivate, and enable others to contribute toward organizational success.

One of the interviews I did early on in the pandemic was with philanthropist and retired successful entrepreneur Richard Jaffe, coauthor with his daughter Charly Jaffe of the book *Turning Crisis Into Success: A Serial Entrepreneur's Lesson on Overcoming*

*Challenge While Keeping Your Sh*t Together.* During our conversation, he described the difference between the two roles in this way: "Managers get their authority from above and a leader gets their authority from below, their followers. If you want to know who the leaders are, just look at who people are following" (2019).

In simple terms: Managers have people who work for them. Leaders have people who follow them.

Managers create circles of power. Leaders create circles of influence.

Influence is *not* to be confused with power or control. It's *not* about manipulating others to get your way. While one *COULD* call it "power"—and yes, the elements of leadership have been about taking charge—again, there is a subtle difference.

Managers create circles of power. Leaders create circles of influence.

In today's business world, I believe it's about hyper-empowering your people. You must trust them, and as a leader, you must let them know you trust them. This is how you have influence. A leader's ability to have influence with his/her teams is based on trust. I call this kind of trust "the foundation of your sphere of influence."

You may be asking yourself, what is a sphere of influence? Do I have one? And if I do, how do I go about building it?

Yes, you have one, even if you don't realize it.

There are three very important components to building your sphere.

1) Be a giver.
2) Be a connector.
3) Be consistent, which means you walk the walk and talk the talk.

The most successful people in business are the ones who are the most connected. And being a giver and a connector are very similar in some respects.

Being a giver could be as simple as, "What can you do to make someone's life a little easier, either through your connections or your flexibility?" Even giving compassion and empathy can go a long way.

Being a leader is about being a connector! Position yourself as a resource, offer a potential solution, or connect people to others who can be a resource or offer a solution.

Remember: Relationships are everything. Do you know much about the people you work with, like their spouse or partner's name, children's names, ages, their hobbies, their passions? Perhaps you've learned MORE than you wanted to because of COVID-19 and everyone video conferencing over virtual platforms from their homes.

Lisa Gable is currently the CEO of FARE, a food allergy research and education organization. Prior to this role, she was the innovative businesswoman who was usually brought in when organizations were headed in the wrong direction, ready to give up. Gable has been called a "turn-around mastermind." For more than thirty years, she's been saving companies, government agencies, and nonprofit foundations from ruin by solving their most complex problems that others hadn't or couldn't solve. And she credits a lot of her success to her ability to build relationships and be a connector.

Just as Gable was taking over the reins of FARE, she, like many leaders, had to deal with the pandemic. During my podcast interview with her, I learned that she stayed connected to her new employees by treating every one of them, and their families, as members of the team; she got to know all of them personally. One such way was through a virtual arts and crafts show. For two weeks, Lisa asked all the children of her employees to send her their pictures and videos, even of them singing songs. She then sent the entire collection back out to everyone with an inspirational message. Lisa found a way to connect everyone. Her actions and her words showed her employees that she truly cared about them. She made them feel special.

As Theodore Roosevelt once said: "No one cares about how much you know, until they know how much you care."

When you are known as a connector, your sphere of influence grows because you are making it about them, and not about you. When you are consistent—and your actions speak louder than your words—when you are walking the walk and not simply talking the talk, when you are giving and connecting, not only are you tapping into building your sphere of influence, but you are tapping into your authentic leader within.

Presence

Leadership, authenticity, and presence are very closely intertwined. When you see someone with presence, you know it. You *feel* it. You also know when it's *not* there.

Our new hire arrived at Channel 5. I always took great delight in welcoming new team members into our TV family; I think I wanted them to feel welcome since I knew what it felt like to *not* feel welcome.

As I looked across the newsroom towards this young man there was something special about him. He had this aura, an energy that seemed to exude from his being. I had this feeling—call it a premonition, intuition, it matters not what you call it—I said to myself, *This man is going to take Peter Jennings's place one day.* Jennings, at that time, was the anchor of *World News Tonight* on ABC.

Jennings died from lung cancer in 2005. For the next nine years, there would be other talented journalists who filled that chair, but in September of 2014, my friend's dream—and my premonition—came true as he was named sole anchor of *World News Tonight with David Muir.*

David's intelligence, leadership, keen perception, and connection with viewers have made this broadcast highly successful, and it continues to dominate the ratings night after night.

During our few short years working together at NewsCenter 5, David and I became fast friends. We often co-anchored newscasts together, and there were many times the station asked us to attend various charity events in the community to represent WCVB.

One such black-tie event was the Annual Gala for the Boston Public Library. When we arrived, we felt like we were on the red carpet in Hollywood. With bulbs flashing everywhere, the local paparazzi swarmed us. We were all smiles and just laughed that this was happening. But honestly, I think it was, in part, David's charisma and magnetism that garnered so much attention. He had presence.

When I was first talking with my mentors about what I could teach people, one of them said to me that I could teach people how to have presence. *Me? Teach someone how to have presence? How would I do that? Did I even have it myself?* So many questions filled my head. It never dawned on me that I had presence, let alone would know how to teach others to have it. As I began to own more of me, I realized I did have presence, and yes, I did know how to teach it too.

One of my biggest corporate clients brought me onto the coaching roster to work with their top-level executives and leaders who for one reason or another were told they needed more executive presence.

The Center for Talent Innovation, a New York nonprofit research group, did a survey with senior executives, and it revealed that executive presence accounts for 26 percent of what it takes to get promoted (Goudreau 2012). That, to me, is a pretty big piece of the pie, and yet many have no idea how to define what presence is. All successful leaders have presence, but what it is and how one gets more of it often eludes people.

Whether I'm working one on one with a client or leading a workshop on the topic of presence, I begin by asking the questions: What is presence? Is it some kind of magic? Who has presence? Public figures, celebrities, politicians, anyone?

We make a list, and their answers are always interesting. Of course, there are the usual names of President Obama, his wife Michelle, Oprah, athletes such as LeBron James, Michael Jordan, Tom Brady, and many more. But what is "it" that gives these individuals the distinction of having presence? What characteristics do they share?

Sometimes naming those traits—putting actual words to them, defining them—is a challenge, but if you don't know what presence is, nor what it looks like, or can't describe it, how can you possibly emulate it?

Great actors have presence. They command the stage even before they have said a single line of dialogue.

Dictionaries define presence as exuding personality that is steeped in poise and confidence, or even as having a supernatural spirit—a divine spirit—to it. I think it's all of those and more.

It's the "it" factor. It's the energy that someone exudes.

Presence can be large for some. It can look and feel like a billion-watt nuclear reactor! We've all seen people with that kind of aura. It can also be intimate and calming. I think of Maya Angelou, whom I interviewed many years ago before her passing. Her calming presence was so amazing. It was quite beautiful.

There are differing theories on whether we are born with presence or not, whether it's nature or nurture. Either way, I believe we have a say in our presence or lack of it. It comes down to the choices we make, the actions we take or fail to take. It is our communication skills, our verbal delivery and/or our nonverbal cues, our body language, our attire and grooming, which say a lot about our presence without a single word coming out of our mouths.

All of this is within your control. These are your "tools," and if you use them well, they can and do transform your life, leading to more presence and being the leader within.

Even though clients have often come to me to work on their executive presence or communication skills, invariably the topic of leadership surfaces in our sessions. As I began working with people on how to be better leaders, I was often struck by the fact that I knew so much about how to be a leader, and yet, as I think back on my career and some of my years in television, I'm not sure I allowed my own leader within to shine through.

In hindsight, I know "it"—she—was there, but was it because of the imposter syndrome, my own lack of confidence, that I didn't feel I had a voice worthy of being heard because I didn't wear the journalist "Big J" on my chest? Perhaps it was a combination of all of it, those limiting beliefs.

There were some people who I felt were true leaders at our television station. They not only had presence, but they were genuinely authentic. What I saw of them on TV and how they behaved when off the air were one in the same. There were others who weren't in the spotlight that had those same qualities. They all owned their own leader within.

I allowed the leader within me to rise up. I began to OWN ME.

One of the best compliments I ever received about my work as an anchor and reporter was from a viewer who said to me, "Even though you often have to deliver bad news, the way you share it with us makes me feel like everything is going to be okay. I trust you."

I believe the viewing audience and others I worked with saw me as a leader, but it wasn't until I left that environment that I saw it in myself. I allowed the leader within me to rise up. I began to "own me."

Time To Reflect:

It's very important as you reflect on these questions to remember there are no right or wrong answers. These are *your* answers. And if you are willing to be honest and vulnerable, they can be valuable in guiding you to become the leader within.

Make a list of at least three people who you believe to be leaders and why you think so. What qualities do they bring to the table that you admire? Do you believe you have those qualities within you, and if you do, are you allowing them to rise to the surface? If not, why not?

What are your strengths, and what do you think are your "development opportunities"?

For example:

- When assigning tasks, I consider people's skills and interests.
- I handle crises and rapidly changing situations smoothly.
- I create a climate of open communication and trust at all levels.

Make a list of the leaders who have impacted your life and how. Was it their intelligence (IQ), their technical expertise, or their emotional intelligence (EQ)? And which do *you* need to work on?

Who are the people you believe have "presence" and why?

Are you a giver and a connector? Are you consistent in your words and actions? Which do you need to work on?

8

Is it a Wish or a Dream?

Go confidently in the direction of your dreams.
Live the life you've imagined.

~ Henry David Thoreau

Make the Commitment

One Sunday morning while sipping my coffee, I began listening to a Joel Osteen message. I always find his sermons inspirational. They strengthen my faith, and that's saying a lot. As a minister's daughter, I was comfortable with my father's way of preaching, and he was very good at it, if I may be so bold as to say so. His style of preaching, his voice, his messages were valuable. So, perhaps, I have always been a bit prejudiced when listening to other ministers. Only a few have spoken to me in a way that has resonated. Joel Osteen is one of them.

On this particular morning, his topic was about turning your dreams into reality and what you are willing to do to make it happen. He suggested—and I completely agree with him—that there is a difference between *wishing* something would happen and *dreaming* it into reality. Osteen, in 2018, said:

"The difference between a dream and a wish: A wish is something you just hope it happens, but a dream you put actions behind. Wishing isn't going to get you anywhere. The people that succeed don't always have the most talent. They simply want it more than others. Being passive and indifferent will keep you from your destiny" (6/17/18).

Everyone's destiny is different. Everyone's definition of success is different as well.

According to various online dictionaries, success can be defined as accomplishment, earning or attaining popularity and/or profit, achieving goals and prosperity.

Accomplishment. Attainment. Achievement. Every single one of those descriptions requires action. One cannot be passive or indifferent.

Success is not an accident.

No, it may not be easy, and yes, some luck may come into play, but the difference between a wish and a dream boils down to this: A lot of people may have a vision—a wish—but it's another thing to implement it—a dream. Wishing isn't going to get you anywhere, and as Joel Osteen says, it takes action.

So, the question we all need to ask ourselves is how committed are we to making this dream a reality? What actions are we willing to take?

I've known a lot of people who had a lot of big ideas, big dreams, but the dreams remained wishes because these individuals lacked a very important component to bringing them to fruition: initiative. With initiative comes action.

I'm reminded of a young man who left a lucrative job because he wanted to write for a living, which is both admirable and courageous in many respects. He certainly had the wish part down, but one day I asked him what he was doing to make that wish a dream, a reality. Out of his mouth came "reasons" why he felt he was *not* able to move the dial. Many of them were absolutely legitimate reasons (an ex-wife and three children to support), but what I also heard was that he had no plan. There were no action steps being taken that would seriously transform his dream into a reality. And as such, it simply remained a wish.

A chiropractor friend of mine and I were discussing the topic of feeling like being on the precipice of something great happening professionally. He jokingly said he'd felt that way for thirty years! He kept hoping, wishing, believing his big break would come someday. I asked him what he was doing, or had done, to bring about realizing this dream and turning it into reality. He gave many of the standard responses of having responsibilities, running his own business, two kids, and taking care of his family. But then he paused, took a deep breath, and in a vulnerable moment said he thought that perhaps his own self-esteem and self-worth issues were at the root truth of what stopped him from really making a bigger name for himself. Sure, he'd written a few articles, but often would say to himself, "Why would anyone care about what I think?" or "Who do I think I am to deserve that kind of success?"

It sounded all too familiar. Imposter syndrome had once again held someone back from manifesting their dreams.

Maybe many of you have even experienced similar situations and emotions. Perhaps we all have to one degree or another. Sometimes life gets in the way, or we get in our own way, or both.

It's your path.
Your life.
Your dream.

I could sit here and write that I know the secret of how to help transform your wishes to dreams, yet your responsibilities and the actions you must take are yours alone. I don't know what the answers are, for you. I don't think there is *one* magic bullet, nor a one-size-fits-all approach. There is no right or wrong path to get there. It's your path. Your life. Your dream.

What I can share with you is what I tell my clients: The path you choose is most likely not going to be easy. Your responsibilities and commitments may remain the same, but if you truly believe in your dream, you will find a way—if you are committed and willing to give it 100 percent.

Now, 100 percent doesn't mean you drop everything in your life and leave your responsibilities behind. What it means is you make a 100 percent commitment to work at your dreams.

I also believe that you must believe your dream can happen, that it *will* happen, and that you have every right to give it the full commitment it deserves. You must give yourself permission to take the initiative, to take action. Often people simply don't give themselves permission to make that 100 percent commitment.

Commitment, initiative, and action may mean making sacrifices; there are only twenty-four hours in a day, so you may have to give up doing something in order to put in the time. Even if it's simply doing one thing a day, one step at a time, give yourself permission to do it.

It's also important to ignore the naysayers and find your supporters. They will help keep you accountable. Now, if those naysayers are people in your own inner circle, no doubt that adds another layer of challenge, but if they are truly in your corner, they will want to help you achieve your dream. Maybe you can even make them a part of the process in some way.

For those who find making that 100 percent commitment and being persistent easy, more power to you, congratulations! But if you are struggling, and it's because of the naysayers in your life, find other mentors who can help motivate you.

There will be days when your commitment to your dream will wane, and you won't have the persistent drive you wish you had. You may feel less than motivated but remember that no one is motivated all the time. Show yourself grace through your tests, but always stay the path of pursuing your dream.

If you ever do feel like giving up, this is when you need to stop and ask yourself: Why do I feel like giving up?

- Is it a fear of failure or of being rejected in some way?
- Are you afraid of succeeding? Yes, people are sometimes afraid they will succeed! Mostly because of the responsibilities that may come with achieving that dream.
- Is the risk to keep going just too high a price to pay? Or would your life be better if you did let go?
- Are you exhausted because it's taking more time and/or longer than you thought or had planned or because obstacle after obstacle seems to come your way?
- Or could you even be bored with this dream? It happens. You start out chasing something only to discover maybe it's not your dream after all. Maybe it was someone else's dream for you.

If you can figure out the "why" you want to give up, and the "why" you should keep going, you will have more clarity. That clarity may also give you permission to let go of a dream. It's okay. It is not a failure if you have really thought it through and can let it go without any regrets.

"Knowing when to let go of a dream is just as important as knowing when to follow one". (2021, 8) Wise words from Jamie Kern Lima, who believed with every fiber of her being that she had to pursue her dream. She was a former TV reporter who co-founded IT Cosmetics in her living room, and finally, after years and years of rejections, sold it to L'Oréal for $1.2 billion. Jamie's extraordinary journey as a self-made entrepreneur, of never giving up on her dream, is revealed in her memoir *Believe It: How to Go from Underestimated to Unstoppable.*

Jamie gave herself permission to never give up on her dream, nor herself. And so did Patty Aubery. Patty went from being a secretary, to a *New York Times* best-selling author, to running the first billion-dollar publishing empire.

Patty is president of the Jack Canfield Training Group, as in the *Chicken Soup for the Soul®* series of books. For eighteen years, she published more than 230 titles in that series, coauthoring fourteen of them. In 2020, Patty published *Permission Granted: Discover How Life Changes When You Give Yourself Permission.*

Patty was a guest on my podcast, and we talked extensively about what it means to give ourselves permission. "I always say, get out of your logical brain… act as if you have a magic wand. And if you did, what would your life look like? What would you be doing? What do you love to do? And if you don't even know what that is, then it's time to work deeper and deeper" (2021).

Once you figure that out, Patty goes on to say, the next step is to declare that big dream out loud because then the pressure is on. "Now you have to show up. It's a new level of responsibility. It's a new level of commitment. It will be scary. But if you're not scaring yourself, you're slacking."

Patty also believes that once you share your dreams and your vision with other people, there's always someone who is willing to help, if you give yourself permission to ask.

So, share that dream. Ask for help. Take action. Create a plan. The truth is, sometimes we don't know what the steps are to create that plan of action. When I started my business, I had no clue. I didn't know anything about how to put a business plan in place, and the one I did put together was blown out of the water in the first three months of operating. At least I had a starting point, and I was willing to evolve and grow with each lesson learned.

I made the commitment to learn. I surrounded myself with smart, good people to guide me, and I was vulnerable with each of them, being totally honest that I needed help to make this dream come true. I gave myself permission to ask for help. I also relied on all my experiences and knowledge, trusting that I would figure it out.

Our dream and our definition of success may mean different things at different stages of our lives. It evolves with us. But we must make the commitment to the journey.

In my first career as a high school music teacher, success was teaching students not only about singing and how to use their voices, but how to connect with an audience and why music was important in life. We gave concerts where each group performed, including our fun swing-show choir. Everyone walked out smiling.

My next job—to pay the bills—was as a clothing salesperson. Success meant selling more than $100K of merchandise each year, putting me into the company's elite $100,000 Club.

Then I found television. During my twenty-eight years in broadcasting, success was all about getting the exclusive interview, producing and writing a compelling story, and beating the competition with the best ratings, night after night, week after week.

In my current role as an executive communications coach, success looks different. What brings me the most feelings of joy and success are when my clients recognize and own the growth in themselves! It's not about me, it's about them. They feel and act with more confidence, can command a room as a leader, or deliver a presentation that knocks it out of the park. They have taken action. They have turned their wish into a dream.

My mother, Mary C. Russell, was a medical social worker and often worked with rehab patients. She would ask them to ask themselves these important questions:

1) Do I need to start doing something? If so, what?
2) Do I need to stop doing something? If so, what?
3) Do I WANT to start or stop doing that "something"? In other words, what am I willing to do differently?

Moving from a wish to a dream, a successful reality, often requires making different, sometimes difficult, choices in life, and we are often not gracious about change, especially the older we get.

As I've evolved, so too has my definition of success. I believe success is about continuing to grow, to learn, to push toward new experiences, to be my best authentic self.

It takes commitment. It takes initiative. It takes drive. It takes perseverance.

Getting to the White House

One of my biggest career highlights as a journalist took plenty of perseverance and persistence, and I am so glad I never gave up on that dream!

I had finally done it! I got perhaps the biggest exclusive interview of my television career. It was February 20, 2013, and all I could think of in that moment was, *Oh my gosh! I am actually here.* I was in the Diplomatic Reception Room, in the White House, awaiting President Barack Obama's arrival for my one-on-one interview. It had taken four years to get there.

When President Obama took office in 2009, he made history as the first Black president of the United States, and I wanted to talk to him. No matter your politics, interviewing a sitting president is an honor. The only way I knew how to get an interview with him was to reach out to the Media/Communications Office at the White House. But, no surprise, there was only a generic email address. No specific name of someone I could write to, and no phone number to call either. That office must receive hundreds, if not thousands, of emails a week with requests like mine from reporters all over the country, maybe even the world. How would my email ever get noticed? I didn't know, but I figured I had nothing to lose by asking. Thus began four years of my sending blind emails to the White House Press Office—mind you, with no replies that I can recall.

Believe it or not, there were people in the newsroom who made fun of me for sending off my requests. "There goes Liz, writing to the White House again!" They only knew of my emails because of meetings that were held in which we would each need to share an update on some of the stories we were working on. I was often going after someone who would be considered an exclusive. I got quite a few during my tenure at WCVB, and I'm proud of that. However, those stories often took much longer to secure than most and a lot of more time and energy too in trying to connect with the right people and persuade them to speak to me. Persistence was required.

By this time, President Obama had been elected to a second term. I still had no interview; no word (radio silence) from the Press Office at the White House.

That is until one day I not only got a reply to one of my numerous emails, but it came with an actual name too! Doug knew me from Boston and my work at Channel 5 and said he wanted to make this happen. *What? Really? He wants to help me get my exclusive interview with the president? Wow!*

I don't recall how much time passed from when I received that email to when I actually got the green light that it was a "go," but once it was a "yes," there were only about forty-eight hours between that confirmation and when I would be headed to Washington, D.C.

A team was assembled that included the news director, an executive producer, and a couple of other folks. Although none of them would be going with me, we immediately got to work on what I would ask the president. Of course, the White House had the topics that they requested I discuss with the president, some of his agenda issues, but I had my own questions too. Plus, I was only going to be granted a short amount of time with him, around four or five minutes, yet I was going to be expected to create four new stories and do four live shots out of that one interview—one story for each newscast that night at 5:00 PM, 5:30 PM, 6:00 PM, and the 11:00 PM show.

On top of that, those forty-eight hours before hopping on a plane to D.C. were filled with all kinds of background checks and security measures that I had to pass in order to officially be allowed to go. And let's not forget this important question: What would I wear for such an occasion? I immediately called Sarah, my personal shopper at Saks Fifth Avenue. She knew that I rarely, if ever, bought anything at full price, but I didn't care that time around. I wanted to find the perfect outfit, whatever it cost, and I did—a beautiful black brocade Dolce & Gabbana suit. Thankfully, the price tag didn't break the bank, and only one minor alteration was needed. They rushed it through so I would have it in time. It still hangs in my closet today. I refuse to get rid of it.

Although my interview wasn't scheduled until 2:30 in the afternoon, my videographer Steve and I had to arrive by 8 o'clock in the morning. With a lot of camera and editing gear in tow, there were many security measures we had to go through to even be allowed onto the grounds.

Once we passed through all the layers of security, I learned that the Press Office had also invited a few other reporters from around the country to be there that day to get their few minutes with the president, but I would be the first one to interview him. Talk about pressure. Was I nervous? Of course! But I kept reminding myself of the once-in-a-lifetime opportunity and to stay present in the moment, enjoy every minute of it… or at least do my best to try to enjoy it all, no matter the nerves. And I did enjoy it. A full day of special activities had been arranged for us: a private tour of the White House and meetings with a few key members of the president's administration. The head chef took us through Mrs. Obama's garden, and we even met Bo, the Obama family's Portuguese water dog, on the front lawn.

Then it was time to get down to the real reason I was there. The Diplomatic Reception Room was filled with many of the Press Office staff, and even though my videographer/editor from Boston was with me, we learned it was the White House's videographers who would record the interview, just another security measure on their part.

While much time had been spent preparing my line of questioning, it was important to me to connect with President Obama on some human, personal level right off the bat. But what could that be? How would I first say hello to such a powerful person?

I knew the president and I had at least one thing in common: the islands of Hawaii had been part of both our childhoods. He was born in Honolulu, and my family moved to the Big Island when I was just a year old. I was ready with the perfect opening line.

As President Obama strode into the room and walked toward me, he greeted me with a warm, "Hello, Liz." I responded with, "Hello, Mr. President, or should I say *aloha*?" He gave me a big smile, and we briefly chatted about Hawaii. As nice a moment as that was, I was thinking in the back of my mind, *I hope the clock hasn't started ticking yet with my allotted interview time!*

In most circumstances, I love to do follow-up questions when I'm interviewing someone, but time was of the essence, with not a minute to spare. I intentionally saved one question until the very end, mostly out of fear that if I asked it sooner and the press team didn't think it appropriate, they might cut me off and tell me the interview was over.

"Mr. President, you are not only the president of the United States, but you are the father of two teenage daughters. Which is harder?" Thankfully, with a laugh in his voice and a grin on his face, he answered that he felt lucky. He has two really good young girls. *Whew! What a relief.* I wasn't immediately whisked out of the room. We had shared another nice moment together: our greeting at the start and at our conclusion. It was a nice bookend moment. Ironically, it was those two moments that people who saw all four stories remembered most.

But then, one slight problem had emerged. Unbeknownst to us at the time, the format in which the White House videographers had recorded the interview was different from our editing decks. We would have to have the interview video reformatted so that I could watch the interview, write my stories, and have my videographer edit them in time for at least our first live shot at 5:00 PM. There was a frantic rush to find a machine that would do the transfer, which practically wiped out those couple of hours I thought I had to prepare.

I tried to remember his answers to my questions so I could at least try to sketch out some sort of an outline for my first story, but truth be told, I think this is where my nerves really surfaced, and I felt like I couldn't remember a thing!

Finally, at about 4:15 PM, we got the new transferred video. I quickly reviewed it and wrote my first story, giving my editor about fifteen minutes to edit it so we could be live at the top of the 5:00 PM show. To say it was nerve-racking would be an understatement. I wanted to do such a good job—no, a *great* job! All I could think of was to try to stay calm. *Just breathe, Liz.*

We got through the first live shot, and I immediately began writing story number two for the 5:30 PM newscast. Again, my videographer/editor was feeling the pressure too. One more to go, the 6:00 PM story, before we could take a breath.

We concluded our final live shot and story from the White House lawn for the 11:00 PM newscast. What a day it was! I was exhausted and exhilarated at the same time from our long day. It had been such an exciting experience for so many reasons, including standing in a row with other national correspondents doing their own live shots. I had truly allowed myself to really embrace that experience, nerves and all. It's one I will never forget.

I've always been a hard worker and have taken great pride in my work ethic. Getting this interview proved to me that perseverance and determination do pay off. So too does ignoring the naysayers. So often in life, people either may not believe in us or ridicule us for dreams we may have. It can be challenging to block out the noise at times, but when we do, and we own those dreams, you never know where they may lead. After four years, this dream led me to the White House.

Another Dream

For years, people have been telling me, "Liz, you should write a book." That comment came from friends, clients, workshop participants, and people who were in the audiences of many keynote speeches I delivered. My response was often, "I'd like to. Maybe, someday." But inside my head, I was often thinking, *I have no clue how to write a book. How does one even begin to write a book? What could I possibly say that people would want to read?* All limiting beliefs! How many of us say "maybe" or "someday" to so many things we wish for but hold ourselves back because of that inner critic in our head?

So, for me, initially it was simply a wish. The idea did intrigue me, but I knew I had a lot to learn. Sure, I'd written stories for newscasts, written speeches for the conferences I spoke at, and helped clients rewrite their own content, presentations, and stories. But me, write a book? *Hmm, I'm not sure how to do that.*

I had to first take initiative, act, and gain the knowledge I felt I needed to learn how to do this. I bought and read a lot of books about writing books. Many were filled with very good advice too, but none of them felt exactly right about how I would go about doing it. For example, almost all the so-called experts I read said first write an outline, followed by all your chapter titles, then write a synopsis of each chapter, and then start writing your book. Every time I tried to do that, I felt like I failed at it.

While I did finally come up with a rough outline, possible chapter titles, and even a flow of one chapter to the next, writing a synopsis of each chapter *before* I'd written the chapter was a real struggle for me.

Because of all my years in journalism, my brain works differently. I'm used to synthesizing large amounts of information and then boiling it down to create small, short stories that fit into a news format. I could take large amounts of AP wire copy or a one-hour interview with someone and bring it all together in a one-minute-and-thirty-second story. Going in the opposite direction felt foreign to me.

I needed to write the chapter first and then write the synopsis. I also knew that some of what I thought I wanted to potentially write about would be a very vulnerable experience. I had to give myself permission to be vulnerable and authentic. That, in and of itself, was scary enough.

I gave myself permission to be vulnerable and authentic.

By the summer of 2019, I felt like I had read enough "how to write a book" books to at least attempt to really begin this journey in earnest.

When I first shared the very rough initial draft outline of the book with a literary agent I had once met, she said she was surprised it contained memoir, expecting it to be 100 percent an all-business book. Well, that didn't help my confidence any. I continued to write, nonetheless.

There was a second big-time agent to whom I was introduced, and as much as he liked what I was writing, he said this was not a genre his publishing company dealt with and pointed me in yet another direction. The next person I dared to share any content with also liked it but also said he wanted more of this and more that. At the time, I still wasn't sure of exactly what he meant. Helpful, I guess, but again, I felt somewhat rejected, despite the positive comments I had received along the way.

I at least did one thing the experts suggested: I kept writing, even though it was only snippets here and there.

While I never gave up on writing a full-fledged book, I did put it aside for nearly eighteen months. Life—all its challenges, responsibilities—got in the way. I felt less than motivated, to say the least. See, it happens, even to me! It had been a wish of mine, but not quite a dream yet. I also felt like I was getting off course. So, I stopped writing.

In early 2021, while still in the middle of the COVID-19 pandemic, I not only felt called to get back to it, but I was also ready to do so. I had to do this. I had to finish my book. I made the commitment! One step: getting connected to a writing coach, Shauna Hardy, who I knew would guide me to the finish line. She was not a naysayer. She was one of my supporters!

I bravely shared with her all that I had written thus far, and what was so much fun (yes, fun) was her saying to me, "I want to know about this experience or that story." I now understood what that third agent was trying to explain. I was often bemused at some of the stories she wanted more details on, and I thought, *Really? You want to know about that? Okay, here goes.*

I took action, again. I blocked off time in my calendar specifically for working on this book. I began reworking, rewriting. I felt inspired to keep going. I was on a mission.

Trust me, a lot of the content and titles have changed since I first began this journey in the summer of 2019. I have also evolved personally while writing this book. And, truth be told, when I first began to write this chapter, I didn't know exactly what all I wanted to say. Only that I believed I could turn this wish into a dream. So, at the very moment of writing this sentence, it is more than a wish. I am on my way to making it a dream come true. And if you are reading this, then you know that I did it.

I gave myself permission to take action. I took the initiative to learn how to do this. I made the commitment, carved out a plan, and I found my community of supporters.

And I truly hope that this story alone motivates and inspires you to believe in your dream and find the will, the courage, and the perseverance to bring it into your reality. Say yes to success, whatever that dream is for you. It could be your next chapter.

Time To Reflect:

What is your dream? Maybe you want to start a business, write a book, or make partner in your company or law firm. Maybe it's to find more balance in your life, more peace.

Whatever that dream is, start by answering these questions.

1) If I had a magic wand, what would my life look like? What is that dream?

2) Am I willing to give myself permission to make the 100 percent commitment to turn it from a wish into a dream?

3) And in the words of my mother:

    a) Do I need to start doing something? If so, what?

    b) Do I need to stop doing something? If so, what?

    c) Do I want to start or stop doing that "something"? What am I willing to do differently?

Do you need a little push to start moving toward your dreams? There are courses on BrunnerAcademy.com that could give you the kickstart you need: Dare: To Go for Your Goals and Dare: To Shift, from Procrastination to Motivation.

Reflect on a time in your life when you may have had a naysayer or someone who put you down rather than supported you in your dreams and goals. Did you let it get to you, or did you persevere despite them? What could you have done differently?

Or maybe you didn't listen to the doubters; how did that make you feel that you followed your own voice and you owned your own dreams? I bet it gave you a lot of confidence!

Whose dreams are you supporting? Can you make a list of at least three people you know who are holding onto a dream or a goal? See if you can find a way to show your support.

Not everyone we know and love, whether they are family members or friends, will like every dream or goal we have, but I believe that if they truly care, they will hopefully find a way to support us, even if it means simply saying “good luck.”

Own Your Next Chapter

SECTION THREE

9

What's Next?

Behold the turtle. He makes progress only when he sticks his neck out.

~James Conant

From the Newsroom to the Boardroom

Covering some of the biggest stories, and being a witness to moments in history, was indeed a privilege and an honor.

I'm a sports fan, so I feel fortunate to have had a front row seat to many major sporting events. I was in New Orleans for a week reporting on Super Bowl XXXI in 1997, when the New England Patriots played the Green Bay Packers. Even though the Packers beat the Patriots, 35-21, it's still a highlight to cover such a big game.

This was the only time I would cover a Super Bowl in person and on-site, and I was fortunate that I was working with a group of guys who'd all been there before and were so willing to guide me through the week. I gained experience and knowledge I would continue to use going forward in other major events. And despite the twelve-to-fourteen-hour days, we did manage to find some time to experience some of the New Orleans culture: beignets, beads, and of course, Bourbon Street.

The NBA finals in 2008 between the Boston Celtics and Los Angeles Lakers renewed a storied rivalry between these two teams that has often been called the greatest in the NBA. This was the first time in twenty-one years these two teams were back at it on the parquet for the championship. It was a true historical event. The Celtics won the series 4-2. Once again, I was the only woman on our crew covering this series, and the hours were long, but that's a given when you are on these special assignments. In this case, when we were in LA, I needed to be ready to go live at 2:00 AM Pacific Time in order to be on the air for the *EyeOpener* newscast at 5:00 AM back home in Boston. After that, it was time to go in search of more stories to be live for all the evening newscasts too. Talk about messing with your body clock!

Among all the events I covered throughout all the years, the Boston Marathon was like no other. Most years, I was at the starting line in Hopkinton in the wee hours of the early morning, pre-race, covering all the runners who began arriving by the busload. In addition, one year I climbed into the back of a pickup truck to report on the men's wheelchair race. South African wheelchair racer Ernst Van Dyk had become a fixture on this course. Van Dyk was impressive, to say the least, having won the Boston Marathon a record-holding ten times. Watching him navigate the streets from Hopkinton to Boston was truly memorable.

Up until 2020, the year of the pandemic, the race had always been held in April, on Patriots' Day, a holiday in MA. Schools are closed, and many people take the day off to enjoy the race. The streets are filled with race-watchers all along the 26.2-mile route.

On April 15, 2013, I was living just a couple of blocks from the finish line in the heart of Boston's Back Bay, and the area was bustling with activity like every other year. I wanted to allow plenty of time to get out of the city and head to Needham to our studios for my evening shift: 3:30 PM-11:30 PM. I'd also been on vacation the prior week and had left several stories to be edited while I was gone. I wanted time to check on them before my shift started.

While in the edit suite, all of sudden, I hear frantic loud voices calling, "Where's Liz? We need Liz. There's been an explosion at the finish line!"

It was 2:49 PM. I ran to the newsroom, jumped up onto our small live desk, threw on a microphone and the IFB earpiece that hung at the desk for anyone who had to use it… my hair in a ponytail, with no makeup on, and very little information to share, I went live. That's what happens when it's breaking news. You just go with what you have, what you do know. Producers were constantly giving me tidbits of confirmed information. I was reaching out to my sources too, gathering any relevant helpful details to share with the public.

Two terrorists had planted two pressure-cooker bombs near the marathon finish line. Three people were killed, hundreds more injured, and more than a dozen lost limbs.

I eventually moved to the studio and was joined by my co-anchor, Ed Harding, and for the next twelve-plus hours, along with our team of incredible reporters, we were on the air nonstop. The story was unfolding so rapidly, and it was alarming.

When they brought in the next anchor team to replace Ed and me, I learned that I was not going to be allowed to drive home. The city was in lockdown, especially around Copley Square. A car service would take me back to the city, but when we were about four blocks away, we were greeted by National Guardsmen carrying weapons who told us we could go no farther. I would have to get out of the car and walk home from there. It was after 3:00 AM! We didn't know if there were terrorists on the loose, so I was not about to walk by myself in the dark. Thankfully, one of the condo building's valet guys came to meet me and walked me safely to the front door.

For the next several days, it was all-hands-on-deck, wall-to-wall coverage, 24/7. It seemed as if every hour there was a new crucial development with so many twists and turns. Because of where I lived—overlooking the marathon finish line—when I looked out my windows, all I saw was the aftermath of the bombing. Debris everywhere. Police and armed guards up and down Boylston Street. I'd never seen so much fire power in my life. Dozens of investigators in sterile white suits, walking slowly, hand in hand, on top of the Boston Public Library, scouring every inch of that roof for evidence. A growing memorial of running shoes, flowers, and candles was filling Copley Square. It was all so haunting. I felt I couldn't escape from the horror of it all. I was talking about the bombing every minute I was at work and visually seeing it firsthand when I was finally allowed to go home each night, always having to prove my identity to armed guards, who surrounded the area for days. It was gut-wrenching.

So too was covering 9-11. Tuesday, September 11, 2001. When the first plane struck the World Trade Center, we learned that a man from Needham may have been on American Airlines flight #11. It was now my job to go to his home and see if any family members would talk to us. As my videographer, Isaiah, and I pulled up in our Channel 5 vehicle, the first thing I noticed was a woman sitting on the front porch crying, and she looked to be about seven months pregnant. I told my videographer to let me go talk to her alone first. I simply couldn't even imagine what she must be going through. As she saw me walking toward her, in a desperate voice, she asked, "Do you know anything?" I had little information I could give her that would ease her heartache. I never asked her for an interview. I just couldn't.

My role for the rest of our coverage in the months and years to come was to follow the victims' families. At the six-month mark, I sat down with a group of about a dozen of them in our studio. Tears flowed as they shared stories and pictures of their loved ones, the pain and loss palpable. Some tugged at their wedding rings, moving them up and down their fingers, unsure of whether to leave them on or take them off. There are really no words to express the raw emotion in the room that night.

I followed this same group at year one, two, three, and year five, each time in our studio. Then, on the tenth anniversary, I decided to gather them in my home. So much had happened in their lives. Although some were clearly still struggling with the loss, it was a celebration of life. Being allowed to witness the transformations and next chapters they had created for themselves was a gift.

Many stories were gifts. When I think of it, I recall a few that really stand out for me. One such story was being able to exclusively cover Richard Mangino's double hand transplant. He'd lost his arms and legs due to a blood infection from an undetected kidney stone. Another was James Maki's partial face transplant. Maki had suffered disfiguring burns to his face after falling onto the T's electrified rail.

In 2005, nine days after winning his third Super Bowl championship with the New England Patriots, Defensive Lineman Tedy Bruschi suffered a stroke. And yet, he decided to go back to the gridiron. I had a chance to talk to him in the Patriots' locker room, where he told me his decision to get back to playing football was about getting back to living.

It was an amazing, exciting career, for which I am very grateful. I learned so much along my journey. Some people are surprised I would consider doing anything else as they consider TV "glamorous." Yes, there are some glamorous moments—such as when I hosted Channel 5's Academy Awards Oscar shows; however, most of it is a lot of hard work, just like any other job. The only real difference, I think, is that my role as a news anchor put me on TV every night, which meant that people *saw* me do my job as opposed to just knowing about it.

"How's your retirement?" Ha! I laughed out loud. "Trust me, I have not retired." No, I was too young to retire. I had just left my twenty-eight-year career in TV to launch my own business. In my eyes, all I had done was moved on to my next chapter.

I had re-created myself, yet again, as opposed to re-inventing myself.

I see the difference between the two as re-invention is doing something completely new, totally learning all new skills, whereas re-creation is taking the skills you have, what you are innately good at, and transferring them to something new. Yes, you may also be learning new skills to ADD to your abilities and expertise, but you are knitting them all together to create something exciting.

Many people have found success and re-created next chapters "later in life." (Notice I did not say *old*!) After starting out as a figure skater and then a journalist, it wasn't until age forty that Vera Wang opened her first successful bridal boutique.

Martha Stewart didn't publish her first cookbook until age forty-three. She'd been a stockbroker on Wall Street.

One of Hollywood's most respected stars—and Academy Award winner—didn't hit the big time for years. Morgan Freeman joined the Air Force to become a fighter pilot out of high school, then chose to leave the military to become an actor. His breakout role came at the age of fifty in the movie *Street Smart*.

Chef Julia Child was also fifty when she launched her first cookbook. Before that, she was a copywriter and a spy during World War II. Talk about a next chapter!

At age fifty-two, Ray Kroc bought out the McDonald brothers, believing in expanding the concept of a fast-food chain after having been a salesman for many years. And for Colonel Sanders of Kentucky Fried Chicken, fame didn't come until the age of sixty-one. He'd been a fireman, insurance salesman, and even practiced law for a time.

Each one of them re-created next chapters for themselves.

No matter whether you call it re-creation or re-invention, in my opinion, everyone needs to think about how they are going to re-create themselves for their next chapter.

In this day and age, male or female, no matter how happy you are in your career, how successful you are, no matter your income, I believe we all need to be thinking in the back of our minds, *Hmm, what else might I like to do "someday"? What am I good at? What am I passionate about? How might I be of service to the world?*

The reality is that whether in TV or any other profession, the likelihood of someone staying in one job or even at one company for twenty to thirty years is not the norm in today's society. Some statistics suggest people are changing jobs—even entire careers—every four to five years.

Sadly, in some respects, gone are the days where your value as an employee was primarily linked to your loyalty and seniority. It's just not like that anymore. No more gold watches. No more monogrammed rocking chairs—my gift after ten years at WCVB. That is just not the world we now live in.

We must all think about our next chapter.

But HOW do you identify what that next chapter is and what the road map looks like to get there?

Often, when facilitating a leadership seminar or workshop, I ask my participants three very important questions:

- Do you know who you are? (In other words, do you know what your strengths and weaknesses are? Did you make your list in the reflections exercise in Chapter Five? What are you going to do to work on your weaknesses? Do you truly own your authentic self? And if not, what do you need to do to own who you are?)
- Do you know where you are going? (Do you know how to take your authenticity and turn your wishes into dreams, to have it be your reality? What are those dreams?)
- And do you know how you are going to get there? (What do you need to do to create that next chapter? What action steps do you need to take?)

What are your answers to those questions? That's perhaps one of the first places to start if you are considering a next chapter.

In hindsight, when I graduated from Lawrence University, I was initially unsure of what exactly I would do with my music degree, let alone who I really was, where I was going, or how I was going to get there.

Who knew when I began my professional adult life that I would have so many different chapters? Certainly not me! Back then, I didn't have the mindset I do now about thinking about what else I might do.

As I look back on my path, in many respects, I "fell" into certain jobs. Some call it synchronicity or being in the right place at the right time or the universe calling the shots; I'm simply following its lead.

Maybe because of hard work, dedication, and perseverance, I've been ready to walk through a door that opened when opportunity knocked.

Or all the above.

And yet, through it all—from high school music teacher to retail salesclerk, to award-winning journalist, to entrepreneur—there has been one constant theme: No knowledge is ever wasted.

"Luck is what happens when preparation meets opportunity," is attributed to Roman philosopher Seneca.

Somehow, preparation—my knowledge and experience—met opportunity, chapter after chapter in my life.

My television chapter lasted for twenty-eight years, taking me through three different television markets: Champaign-Urbana, Illinois, the 75th market at the time, then to Tampa, Florida, the 13th market, and onto Boston, Massachusetts, the 6th largest market in the country. I was very proud of that trajectory and the career I had.

Brunner Communications launched in October of 2013, and by the time the calendar clicked into 2014, the company was on a roll. For the first six years, it was amazing. I was working with great clients, who were becoming more confident and successful. Many were very happy and felt the services and coaching offered were invaluable. It resulted in receiving wonderful accolades, for which I am eternally grateful, but it was also exhausting.

I had something to prove, if only to myself.

I basically said yes to every client and every engagement, no matter where it was. I felt like I was on a treadmill and couldn't get off. I was on a plane almost weekly, going somewhere, crisscrossing the country to continue to work with clients one-on-one. More than 95 percent of my business was coaching and meeting with individual clients and/or teams face-to-face. I can only think of a handful of clients I may have turned down, but simply because I was already booked.

Believe me, I am not complaining. I know how lucky I was to have had success early, especially when so many entrepreneurs fail. I also worked very hard for that success.

According to the Bureau of Labor and Statistics, more than half of new businesses fail within the first year. Approximately 20 percent in the first two years, and 45 percent during the first five years. I had something to prove, if only to myself.

As year six started to unfold, truth be told, the work started to slow down just a bit, which was probably a good thing, but it freaked me out! Many of the large corporate clients I had been working with had done some major restructuring. Executive coaching was not top of mind, no matter how successful my clients were.

Many of my coaching friends were experiencing the exact same thing. All of us were trying to comprehend what was going on and what we could do about it. The stock market was doing well. It didn't make sense to any of us. It was comforting, on one hand, to learn I wasn't alone, but disconcerting on the other.

One thing the slow down gave me initially was being able to start my podcast: *How to Live Your Best Life with Liz Brunner.* One of my local videographers, and now my digital producer, Dan, had been pushing me for months, telling me I needed to do this since podcasting was an exploding medium. My response was always, "I don't have time!" It was a wish, but I wasn't sure if I really wanted to commit to making it a dream. I knew if I did commit, I would love it. Interviewing people and sharing their stories was always one of my favorite aspects of my role as a journalist.

By now, thanks to working with my own business coach, Michelle Vandepas, I really had honed in on what was important to me as I continued to grow my company and the vision I had for my life: to teach, motivate, and inspire people to live their best life, whatever that meant for them.

My podcast allows me to showcase stories of people who have also made career transitions, who are owning who they are, giving themselves permission to turn their wishes into dreams, or who have risen above life's circumstances.

I believe, by hearing these stories, listeners to my podcast episodes can say to themselves, "If that person did it, hey, maybe I can too." And the best part about doing my own show, I don't have anyone—a producer, an editor, nor a news director—telling me I can't say or do something, or that I have to stick to fitting my interview into a certain block of allotted time in a newscast. I can do what I want! How liberating and freeing!

The COVID-19 Pivot

And then, it happened. The world began to face an enemy we had never known: COVID-19. A global pandemic that would change the world as we knew it. Come mid-March of 2020, one by one, every in-person workshop and every individual client engagement I had on my calendar through June started getting cancelled. It all came to a screeching halt.

As the months rolled on, and the outlook kept getting bleaker, like many, I began wondering, *How will I keep my company afloat?* Could I even keep it going? I felt like I was back to square one. I was starting my business all over again. I would have to pivot and rebuild my company, create my next chapter, yet again.

My initial goal was simple: How could I be of service to any of my clients? What could I do as a communications coach to help? But coaching of any kind was simply not on the radar, at least not with many of my big corporate clients. If it was a choice between hiring a coach or keeping an employee, well, you know what choice was made, and rightfully so. They vowed to keep the employee.

Even though I had been in business for nearly seven years by then, I still felt like such a newbie. I'd never been through a business crisis before and had no clue what to do. I returned to informational interviews and reached out to other coaches I knew and respected.

I had to pivot. I would have to figure out how to do what I'd been doing in-person, with a videographer, and do it in a virtual world.

My long-range plan had been to create online public speaking courses in the summer of 2021. That goal and timeline quickly shifted, and I accelerated the launch of BrunnerAcademy.com in 2020. It began with some small, short, free courses for the public, like Confidence in a Virtual World, then I created and produced my flagship public speaking course How to Be a Rock Star Public Speaker.

It may sound crazy, but in some ways, I am grateful for the pandemic. At the pace that I was on, I would never have had the time to create my flagship course; I seized the opportunity! I was also able to garner new clients who began to understand that communicating, connecting, and engaging in a virtual world takes a new set of skills they weren't proficient in. Lucky for them, and me, all those skills are in my wheelhouse!

I *know* I'm not alone when I say 2020 was not easy. Many people had it far worse than me. I didn't pay myself any salary for ten months because it was more important to me to keep my team together—to pay them. I needed *their* help to stay afloat. Not every business expert would agree with that approach, and unfortunately, it didn't serve me well when it came time to apply for PPP funding. Because I hadn't paid myself, in the bank's eyes my business was not in business in 2020, no matter how much documentation and proof I gave them that I was and that I had clients. I'm sure I wasn't the only small business owner that faced such a negative response.

Nor have I been the only one who has been forced to pivot and re-create a next chapter as a result of the pandemic, but others I know have also stopped to take stock of their lives and have asked themselves if the job they are in is still right for them. Are their personal lives what they want them to be?

I have a theory that it's not a coincidence that the pandemic happened in the year 2020.

When we heard or saw the numbers 20-20, prior to the pandemic, we might have had only one thought: going to the eye doctor to make sure we had 20-20 clear vision. Looking up at that big eye chart and reading the smallest line we could, proved we had perfect vision.

The pandemic forced us to take a good hard look at ourselves and how we were living our lives. What did we value most? What were our priorities? Were our lives in alignment with our vision or where we wanted and needed it to be?

So many people made decisions to change their lives in one form or another. According to the Labor Department, in April of 2021, almost four million people nationwide voluntarily quit their jobs. That's the highest single month since they started keeping stats in 2000. People found new jobs, suddenly adopted pets, renovated their homes, and many assessed or reassessed their finances. Being in quarantine, personal relationships were closely examined as well. There were couples who chose to move in together, to marry, and others who chose to split. Others are still figuring it all out, but they are seeking a new chapter because of all that they learned during the pandemic.

Whether the pandemic gave you a chance to rethink your life or you were there already, again, I come back to the notion that we should always be thinking about next chapters.

Professionally, it has nothing to do with whether you are happy where you are or not. It's being open to the possibilities and giving yourself permission to dream.

Jenny Blake was once the career development program manager at Google, yet she wanted to stretch her wings and move into doing other things. No one could believe she would leave such a prestigious job. Thus, upon her departure, she was known as the "girl who left Google."

Today, Jenny is a successful entrepreneur, international speaker, career and business strategist, podcaster, and three-time author—all because she gave herself permission. In her highly successful book *Pivot: The Only Move That Matters Is Your Next One,* she not only chronicles her career transitions, but offers concrete processes people can take when considering making a change.

During our podcast episode together, Jenny talked about how to double down on what's working and what's not. "It's not so much about looking backwards or forwards, but rather giving ourselves permission to do things differently and reinvent a new way forward" (2021).

A thirty-eight-year-old man I know reached out to me because he wanted to learn how I made the transition from TV news to my coaching business. He also wanted my advice. He's been a successful basketball coach in the NBA for many years and knows that he could absolutely continue on that path, and be quite happy, but he's asking himself: What's next? He also feels "called" to do more and be of service in other ways.

It's okay to be afraid because it gives you the opportunity to be brave.

I've also coached clients who started out working with me on one thing and then, somewhere along the way, concluded that they wanted to explore new opportunities. One woman, who was extremely successful in her company, felt ready to leave and move on to her next chapter. However, giving herself permission to leave was harder than she thought it would be, especially since she was also about to be fully vested and felt somewhat financially safe considering an exit.

There is fear, at times, in charting a new path, and very real concerns, financial or otherwise, but don't allow them to keep you stuck.

"It's okay to be afraid because it gives you the opportunity to be brave." That's the tagline of a car commercial I heard many years ago. I don't recall the make nor model, but I remember those poignant words. They have stuck with me all these years.

I encouraged this woman to explore all options, which meant she might need to travel down a couple of paths at the same time to gather information, explore the possibilities, so that she could make the right decision at the right time. She ultimately did leave and has since launched her own business aimed at helping minority women. She is also writing a book about her own experiences. She took the opportunity to be brave.

Being brave is not an innate or inborn trait. It is learned from experience and is acquired over time. Just as we must practice confidence, we can practice bravery by challenging ourselves with new experiences, even if and when we are afraid. (Go back to Chapter Three for a refresher on practicing confidence.)

It's also important to remember that bravery is not the absence of fear, but rather the ability to move on despite being afraid. As I shared with you earlier in this book, if fear was the only reason keeping me from launching my business, that was simply not a good enough reason, at least for me.

Admit you are afraid. Accept that it's okay to be scared. Examine why you have those emotions as some fears are legitimate and can be helpful while others may do more harm than good. Then, focus on what you can control.

Expect the Unexpected

Sometimes we pivot by choice, and sometimes we pivot by circumstance. Next chapters are often thrust upon us, perhaps unexpectedly. Our role at work changes. We may even have been fired. An important relationship ends. We receive a horrible medical diagnosis. A loved one passes away. Our world as we know it suddenly changes.

All of these may feel like small or mini-deaths, and with each of these, we may have to pass through the five stages of grief: denial, anger, bargaining, depression, and finally acceptance. As challenging as it is, it's just part of the natural process of letting go. And we must go through it to get to the other side, to that next chapter.

You may feel powerless to change what has occurred, but you are not without control when the unexpected happens. How you respond and move forward is within your control. As I wrote in a previous chapter, the advice my mother always gave us four children: "It's not what happens to you, but how you handle it that makes the difference."

Your attitude is within your control. How you deal with the "unexpected changes" is within your control. No, it may not be easy, but if you can put yourself into what I call the "witness space" and ask: What are the lessons to be learned from this situation? Do I need to take responsibility for anything that may have happened? As Jack Canfield said in Chapter Three, we have to take 100 percent responsibility for where we are in our life.

In the event of a death of a loved one or an unforeseen medical condition, perhaps that was completely out of your control, but how you move forward with your life *is* in your control.

Life certainly didn't turn out the way Retired Master Sergeant Cedric King thought it would. He'd done one tour of duty in Iraq, and in 2012, this elite Army Ranger was on his third tour in Afghanistan, in one of the most dangerous parts of that war-torn country. King's life changed in a matter of a moment when he stepped on an IED, an improvised explosive device. Eight days later, he woke up in Walter Reed Memorial Hospital severely injured and with both of his legs amputated.

As King recounted his story on my podcast, he shared with me that every service member raises their right hand and takes that oath to defend our country's flag, knowing that this very flag could be draped over them someday. Cedric said, "They [the service members] are prepared for it, however, one never actually thinks it's going to happen to them" (2021).

This was not what he planned for his life. During his darkest days in the hospital, he contemplated ending it all, but he told me he thought that was too selfish, and that somewhere deep within his being, he was being called to a new chapter.

King went on to get his college degree, which he never felt he was smart enough to do. He is now a runner and has competed and finished the New York City Marathon twice and the Boston Marathon five times on his specially designed running blades, along with the Half Ironman. King travels the world sharing his motivational story and is also an author of the powerful book *The Making Point.*

Retired Master Sgt. King took control of his life. He found the stamina to meet the obstacles and overcome them.

"The goal of living is to be able to absorb all of the pain of life and lose none of the joy."

Another pearl of wisdom my mother shared often with my brothers and me.

We can choose to never lose the joy. We can choose to be resilient, despite all hardship.

Life is going to throw us obstacles. There will be struggles, and no one is immune. Sometimes answers don't come easily, and we have to hold the tension of uncertainty. Patience if often required, so too is what I call "positive expectancy."

Dorie Clark is the author of several books, including *Entrepreneurial You; Reinventing You: Define Your Brand, Imagine Your Future; The Long Game;* and *Stand Out,* which was named the number one Leadership Book of 2015 by *Inc.* magazine. A former journalist and presidential campaign spokeswoman, Dorie has been called by *The New York Times* an "expert at self-reinvention and helping others make changes in their lives." In her book *Reinventing You,* she offers a road map for that next phase of your journey. I've gotten to know Dorie, and she's been a guest on my podcast.

We talked about how every career path she was interested in had literally been disrupted in the past twenty years. And yet, because she has adapted and pivoted when the unexpected happened, she has been very successful as an entrepreneur, marketing strategist, executive coach, adjunct professor at Duke University, and prolific writer for the *Harvard Business Review* and *Forbes*. "If you are able to tap into unique skills or abilities that you have cultivated or that leverages experiences that you have had, I think that that is quite meaningful because it means that you are adding something to the world that wouldn't be there otherwise" (2020).

We are the writers, producers, and directors of our lives.

Remember, no knowledge is ever wasted. We are the writers, producers, and directors of our lives. Who you are, with all your unique talents, is a gift from God; what you do with those gifts and talents is up to you.

Time To Reflect:

As you think about your re-creation journey, consider what experiences, skills, and abilities you have as "knowledge." Begin to think about how you can use them to create a next chapter that you feel fulfills your purpose. Challenge yourself to think "outside the box."

What skills do you now see as transferable? How can you now leverage them and offer them to the world in a way that gives your life meaning and adds value?

10

My Next Chapter

Life is a dance. Mindfulness is witnessing that dance.

~ Amit Ray

No Knowledge is Ever Wasted

Whether re-inventing, or simply re-creating, I think one of the biggest hurdles to get past is giving yourself permission to simply be brave enough to consider a next chapter and what that may look like. We all have skills and talents that we don't even acknowledge or give ourselves enough credit for.

No knowledge is ever wasted. So, explore the possibilities, and never sell yourself short.

Had I not explored how I could use my talents, the gifts that I believe I have been blessed with and the skills that I have honed, I wouldn't be where I am today.

It also takes courage.

In the words of Anais Nin, "Life shrinks or expands in proportion to one's courage."

Given the personal stories of challenges and obstacles I have shared with you in this book, it may surprise you that I am a very private person. It's taken courage for me to open myself up and be vulnerable. And yet, every time I do, my life expands in meaningful ways.

And as I write these words, I find myself yet again moving into my next chapter. It took me a long time to give myself permission to turn more wishes into dreams and to truly own even more of who I am, who I feel I am on the inside, and allow the world to see it and know it on the outside.

In Chapter One, I told you that skydiving had been on my bucket list. And as I move into this next chapter, I am taking on yet another bucket list challenge.

Dancing into my Next Chapter

I'm sitting on the couch, alone, smiling from ear to ear, even laughing out loud. I'm watching one of my favorite TV shows, *Dancing with the Stars,* on ABC. I've watched every season since 2005 when it first premiered. I love the elegance, the choreography, and the body's movement. I think I have always had a secret passion to be a dancer—even more so than a singer, which is odd considering all the vocal training and singing I have done in my life! So, when I watch this show, I imagine what that would feel like, to be able to move like that… to be so free... to express myself so authentically.

The professional dancers and celebrities on the show make it look so effortless, and yet, many of the contestants admit that it is not as easy as it looks! And it doesn't matter if they are professional athletes or if they have had some dance experience in their life, they must work very hard day in and day out to make it to the next round.

I've been fortunate to interview many powerful people, including celebrities, and covered many incredible, amazing stories, but truth to be told, when I tell people what one of my all-time favorite stories is, it often surprises them. While I have been to the live show of *Dancing with the Stars* once—I took my mom for her birthday one year—I most likely will never actually compete on the show. (Then again, never say never!) But I did have my own *DWTS* dancing moment.

One of my favorite professional dancers on *DWTS* was Tony Dovolani. His choreography, elegance, energy, and smile lit up the dance floor, no matter who the celebrity was that he was partnered with. While the show is done live in Los Angeles, Tony lived in Connecticut, and I wanted to do a story with him. I asked, and he said yes! It so happens he was going to be back home for only a couple of days in the middle of the show's run, but he was willing to meet with me. I knew I had to maximize my time with him and that I would probably end up writing at least two, if not three, stories from our time together. One of those stories would be him teaching me a dance routine.

My videographer Jason and I drove to Connecticut to Tony's home, interviewed him, spent time with his family, and then we were off to one of the Fred Astaire Dance Studios he was associated with. We had one more hour together, in which he would teach me a thirty-second choreographed tango. My videographer set up two cameras to capture it all.

First came the teaching and learning of the steps. Watching Tony's creative juices flow into designing a routine on the spot was fascinating. I admit, I didn't feel so graceful, but I was enjoying every minute. Yes, I took a few ballet lessons as a little girl, and living in Hawaii I'd learned the hula, but that's the extent of my dancing experience. Tony was so encouraging, but he also wanted me to come out of my shell, to allow for more self-expression, and to be more authentic—so hard!

If you are a frequent watcher of the show, you will often hear the judges say to the celebrity contestants to open up, to allow their authenticity to rise to the surface. Besides the beautiful dancing, that's one of the things I love most about the show. The journey, the transformation that often takes place within a contestant as a result of getting in touch with their inner being, owning who they are, and celebrating that newfound freedom, physically and emotionally.

Finally, it was time to change out of my lululemon workout attire and into my dancing dress for the finished routine.

What can I say? Dancing with a champion ballroom dancer is unlike anything I had ever experienced before. His strength, athleticism, and ability to lead me around the floor with perfect precision and control was a thrilling experience. I knew from that moment on that someday I must take ballroom dance lessons. I didn't know when, but I made a promise to myself that I would.

That time is now. With the world coming out of the pandemic and becoming fully vaccinated, I went in search of a dance instructor. I finally found one. Andriy Vitenko is twenty-six-years-old, from the Ukraine, and a competitive dance champion in his own right.

I'm truly enjoying my lessons. They've become the highlight of my week. I'm filled with joy and laughter with every style of dance. So far, I'm learning the tango, rumba, samba, swing, waltz, and cha-cha, but I have to admit, I feel like I am learning a foreign language. In addition to using muscles I don't normally use, my brain is trying to keep up remembering the steps. We use my iPhone to video portions of my lesson so I can practice at home.

Allow your heart, mind, body and soul to connect - own all of you.

You know by now the importance I place on practice. Earlier in the book, I talked about how important it is to practice any speaking remarks out loud because of the muscle memory that happens between your brain and your mouth. I'm still waiting for the muscle memory to kick-in from my brain to my feet! But I guess it does have to travel all 5'7" of me to get there as opposed to the four inches from my brain to my mouth.

I have a lot to learn, but thankfully, I am getting better, little by little, with each lesson. At least Andriy makes me feel like I am! Don't worry, I have no plans to run off and turn pro, but I do feel like, with each step I take, I'm allowing my heart, mind, body, and soul to all connect. I'm owning all of me. I am dancing my way into my future.

So, as much as I love what I am doing right now—being of service, helping people find their own voice so they can live their best life—I'm still thinking: What is my NEXT chapter?

"No knowledge is ever wasted in the good Lord's sight," said my grandmother. I feel, once again, instinctively, the good Lord has plans for me to fulfill even more of my purpose. There is more for me to do in this world. Whatever it is, it begins with me owning more of who I am.

When I was a guest on Jenny Blake's podcast *Free Time,* she asked me a question that she poses to every guest: "If you could give listeners permission to drop something, or do something differently, if you could just write them a permission slip, what would it be for?"

My immediate response: "Own who you are! Give yourself permission. Forget about what other people's expectations are of you, forget about some of the expectations of yourself, and give yourself permission to be who you are, your best self."

In the words of Joseph Campbell, "The privilege of a lifetime is being who you are."

I invite you to move toward the truth of who you are. Celebrate every part of you. Take your authenticity, your dreams, and allow yourself to create your next chapter. Live your best life, for you.

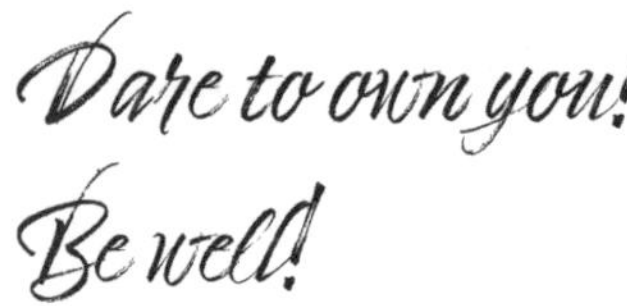

The End

AFTERWORD (SECOND EDITION)

On behalf of all those who contributed to this book (through quotes and anecdotal proof) and to the future you who is forging a new chapter with bravery and authenticity, I want to thank you for dedicating time to explore what it means to dare to own who you are and for reflecting on your own journey of self-discovery. Although our stories and experiences may be different, we may share similar feelings or situations that helped you to see yourself more clearly and will empower you to dust off your dreams and to trust yourself more.

I also hope that you took my Grandmother Chacko's quote to heart, "No knowledge is ever wasted." If you persevere in looking at your experiences, personal and professional, through that lens you will continue to see that all of your experiences that seem unrelated actually are connected! This lens is incredibly valuable when it comes to how to look at the future of work. I believe the future of work is changing in many ways and perhaps you do too; maybe that's even why you chose to read this book.

If you are experiencing these changes and are wondering what your next chapter will be, you may also be curious about how to continue to grow and use this newfound knowledge, confidence, and voice. I invite you to persevere in your quest to live with authenticity by asking yourself not "What do I want in life?" but rather, "How do I want to feel each day?" or "Am I thriving in my work and in my relationships, or am I simply surviving?" We sometimes fear the answers to those questions because this realization may require us to get out of our comfort zone and to make changes, which can be scary; but do not sell yourself short. Do not allow fear to hold you back and do not allow any lingering limiting beliefs to stand in your way. May the experiences shared in this book inspire you to go after what you truly desire, so that you, too, can live your best life.

Writing *Dare to Own You* was an incredible journey of self-discovery for me, and it is a journey that I continue to be on with all of life's ups and downs. But a journey of self-discovery is one with no final destination. It is about growing, one step at a time, and pushing yourself to follow your inner voice. When you practice reflection exercises (like those that I shared through these pages), you realize that the more life you experience, the more you can learn to trust your instincts (which come sometimes as whispers or even a roar) and those will point you in new directions where you will have the chance to own who you are.

My vision for my life is to teach, motivate, and inspire others to live their best life, to help them get unstuck, to help them release their limiting beliefs in order to transform from where they are to where and who they want to be. I am fortunate to be of service in this way as a keynote speaker, sharing my journey, experiences, and expertise on big and small stages, and consulting clients all around the world. I invite you to learn more at my website, lizbrunner.com

Thank you again for taking this journey to live your best life, whatever that means for you. Be well,

Liz

Bibliography

Ackers, Michael & Porter, Grover L. 2003. *Your EQ Skills: Got What It Takes?* New York City: American Institute of Certified Public Accountants.

Aubrey, Patty. 2020. *Permission Granted: Discover How Life Changes When You Give Yourself Permission.* Swedesboro: Kate Butler Books.

Black, Dan. 2012. "What Passion Does for Leaders." San Diego: Dan Black on Leadership. http://danblackonleadership.info/archives/1273

Blake, Jenny. 2016. *Pivot: The Only Move That Matters Is Your Next One.* New York: Penguin.

Brown, Brené. 2013. *Daring Greatly: How the Courage to Be Vulnerable Transforms the Way We Live, Love, Parent, and Lead.* New York: Penguin.

Canfield, Jack. 2013. *Chicken Soup for the Soul* ® series. Cos Cob, CT: Chicken Soup for the Soul Entertainment Inc.

Canfield, Jack. 2015. *The Success Principles ® - 10th Anniversary Edition: How to Get from Where You Are to Where You Want to Be.* New York City: William Morrow Books.

Clance, P. R., & Imes, S. A. 1978. "The imposter phenomenon in high achieving women: Dynamics and therapeutic intervention." *Psychotherapy: Theory, Research & Practice,* 15(3), 241–247.

Clark, Dorie. 2017. *Entrepreneurial You: Monetize Your Expertise, Create Multiple Income Streams, and Thrive.* Boston: Harvard Business Review Press.

Clark, Dorie. 2017. *Reinventing You, With a New Preface: Define Your Brand, Imagine Your Future.* Boston: Harvard Business Review Press.

Clark, Dorie. 2015. *Stand Out: How to Find Your Breakthrough Idea and Build a Following Around It.* New York City: Penguin.

Clark, Dorie. 2021. *The Long Game: How to Be a Long-Term Thinker in a Short-Term World.* Boston: Harvard Business Review Press.

Codyer, Mollie. 2017. "EQ vs. IQ: Who Should You Hire?" Bedford: Hub Recruiting Blog. https://www.hubrecruiting.com/blog/eq-vs-iq-who-should-you-hire

Colapinto, John. 2021. *This is the Voice.* New York: Simon & Schuster.

Comer, Annette. 2010. *Rescue Me! How to Save Yourself and Your Sanity When Things Go Wrong.* Philadelphia: Mass Publishing, LLC.

Craig, Lydia. September 2018. "Are You Suffering From Imposter Syndrome?" Washington, D.C. American Psychological Association, Psychological Association Agenda. https://www.apa.org/science/about/psa/2018/09/imposter-syndrome

Dean, Michael T. February 8, 2020. "Top 6 Reasons New Businesses Fail. " New York City: Investopedia.com.

Dunning III, Harriet Westbrook, & Dunning, Parsons Heddendorf. 2011. *Dunning Chronicles, the family history of some Dunnings and in-laws descended from Morton Dexter Dunning and Stewart Northrup Dunning.* Walden: Waldenhouse Publishers, Inc.

Ferrazi, Keith. 2014. *Never Eat Alone: And Other Secrets to Success, One Relationship at a Time.* New York: Currency.

George, Bill. 2016. *The Truth About Authentic Leaders.* Cambridge: Harvard Business School.

Golden, Gail. (no date) *3 Types of Networking All Successful People Must Master.* Chicago: Gail Golden Consulting.

Goudreau, Jenna. October 29, 2012. *Do You Have 'Executive Presence'?* New York City: Forbes.com.

Helgesen, Sally, & Goldsmith, Marshall. 2018. *How Women Rise: Break the 12 Habits Holding You Back from Your Next Raise, Promotion, or Job.* New York: Hachette Books.

Helpmates Companies. 2018. *Why Preparation is 80 Percent of Career Success.* Los Angeles: Helpmates Companies.

Huber, Liz. 2018. "20 Limiting Beliefs that Mess with Your Dreams. You are Only Confined by the Walls you Build Yourself." San Francisco: Medium. https://medium.com/@refinedliz/20-limiting-beliefs-that-mess-with-your-dreams-b4cfeb2f66ca

Jaffe, Richard, & Jaffee, Charly. 2019. *Turning Crisis Into Success: A Serial Entrepreneur's Lessons on Overcoming Challenge While Keeping Your Sh*t Together.* Cardiff: Waterside Productions

Kay, Katty, & Shipman, Claire. 2014. *The Confidence Code: The Science and Art of Self-Assurance—What Women Should Know.* New York: Harper Business.

Kay, Katty, & Shipman, Claire. 2014. *The Confidence Gap.* Washington, D.C: The Atlantic.

Kimball, Ryder. March 2, 2020. "Jack Welch, the former CEO of General Electric who grew the company's stock price by 4,000%, has died at the age of 84." India: Business Insider. https://www.businessinsider.in/thelife/news/jack-welch-the-former-ceo-of-general-electric-who-grew-the-companys-stock-price-by-4000-has-died-at-the-age-of-84/articleshow/74447153.cms

King, Cedric. 2019. *The Making Point: How to succeed when you're at your breaking point.* Grosse Pointe Farms: Atkins & Greenspan Writing.

Kolber, Petra. 2018. *The Perfection Detox: Tame Your Inner Critic, Live Bravely, and Unleash Your Joy.* Boston: Da Capo Lifelong Books.

Koldotz, Thomas. 2010. *In Extremis Leadership: Leading As If Your Life Depended On It.* San Francisco: Jossey-Bass.

Kramer, Harry. 2015. *Becoming the Best: Build a World-Class Organization Through Values-Based Leadership.* San Francisco: Jossey-Bass.

Lathrop, Richard. 1977. *Who's Hiring Who: How to Find that Job Fast.* Berkeley: Ten Speed Press.

Lima, Jamie Kern. 2021. *Believe IT: How to Go from Underestimated to Unstoppable.* New York: Galley Books.

Love, Tonya. 2016. *3 Tips for Being a Truly Great Leader.* New York: Fortune.

McKinney, Michael. July 18, 2007. *The Importance of Competence.* Pasadena: Leading Blog, Leadership Now.

Neilson, Kate. 2021. "Five Types of Imposter Syndrome (and how to manage them)." Melbourne, Australia: HRM Online Magazine.

Schlafman, Steve. 2018. "Finding Your Own Voice." New York: Schlaf.me. https://schlaf.me/finding-your-own-voice/

U.S. Bureau of Labor Statistics. August 9, 2021. "Job Openings and Labor Turnover Summary." Washington, D.C.: U.S. Department of Labor. https://www.bls.gov/jlt/

For Further Reference

Aubrey, Patty. July 19, 2021. *Live Your Best Life with Liz Brunner.* Podcast Guest, Patty Aubrey. Boston: Brunner Communications.

Blake, Jenny. May 4, 2021. *Live Your Best Life with Liz Brunner.* Podcast Guest, Jenny Blake. Boston: Brunner Communications.

Brunner, Liz. January 2021. How to Be A Rock Star Public Speaker. Online course. BrunnerAcademy.com

Brunner, Liz. May 21, 2021. *Free Time with Jenny Blake*. Episode #15: Preparing to Interview the President with Liz Brunner. Podcast Guest, Liz Brunner. New York City: It'sFreeTime.com

Brunner, Liz. October 2021. Dare: To Find Peace of Mind. Online course. BrunnerAcademy.com.

Canfield, Jack. June 7, 2021. *Live Your Best Life with Liz Brunner.* Podcast Guest, Jack Canfield. Boston: Brunner Communications.

Chamorro-Premuzic, Tomas, & Green, Sarah. July 31, 2014. *HBR IdeaCast,* Episode 416. The Dangers of Confidence. Cambridge: Harvard Business Review.

Clark, Dorie. June 1, 2020. *Live Your Best Life with Liz Brunner.* Podcast Guest, Dorie Clark. Boston: Brunner Communications.

Comer, Annette. June 29, 2020. *Live Your Best Life with Liz Brunner.* Podcast Guest, Annette Comer. Boston: Brunner Communications.

Divine, Mark. March 15, 2021. *Live Your Best Life with Liz Brunner.* Podcast Guest, Mark Divine. Boston: Brunner Communications.

King, Cedric. February 8, 2021. *Live Your Best Life with Liz Brunner.* Podcast Guest, Retired Master Sergeant Cedric King. Boston: Brunner Communications.

Kolber, Petra. July 13, 2020. *Live Your Best Life with Liz Brunner.* Podcast Guest, Petra Kolber. Boston: Brunner Communications.

Osteen, Joel. June 17, 2018. *How Bad Do You Want It?* Episode #766. Houston: JoelOsteen.com

About the Author

An Emmy award-winning journalist, Liz Brunner enjoyed a television career that spanned twenty-eight years and featured many memorable highlights. Along with co-anchoring the #1 rated 6 PM newscast at ABC-TV, WCVB NewsCenter 5 in Boston, she conducted exclusive one-on-one interviews with prominent figures ranging from professional athletes to global political leaders including President Barack Obama as well as cultural icons such as Oprah Winfrey.

In 2013, Liz excitedly embarked upon her next chapter, becoming the CEO and Founder of Brunner Communications, and launched BrunnerAcademy.com in 2020. Both are dedicated to helping people find their authentic voices, tell their stories, and lead with presence. A Certified Professional Coach, expert communications coach, and motivational speaker, Liz is also the host of the multi-award winning *Live Your Best Life with Liz Brunner* podcast, available on all the major directories. Liz guides her guests to share their stories of self-discovery and re-creation. Listeners around the world join in on the journey garnering inspiration from the wisdom shared.

A classically trained vocal performer and former high school music educator, Liz holds a Bachelor of Music degree from the Lawrence University Conservatory of Music. She has performed with the Boston Pops and at professional sporting events for teams including the Boston Celtics, the Boston Red Sox, and the New England Patriots.

Liz can be reached at www.LizBrunner.com and through BrunnerAcademy.com

For more great Empower Press books visit
Books.GracePointPublishing.com

If you enjoyed reading *Dare to Own You* and purchased it through an online retailer, please return to the site and write a review to help others find this book.

DARE TO
OWN
You